LIGHT TRIBE BY PHOS

At Phos, we illuminate more than spaces—we ignite change. We delve beneath the surface of selling beautiful light, driven by an unwavering passion for its transformative power to enrich lives.

Our independent research arm, "Light Tribe", stands as a beacon of exploration, education, and innovation. Through it, we traverse the globe, delivering impassioned lectures to design and educational institutions. Our mission: to rekindle the connection between designers and the natural world, championing biophilic products and practices.

But our vision extends further. We aim to unify all those who yearn to make a difference—to create a formidable force lobbying for real, lasting change in government policy. For in unity lies our strength, and in change lies our future.

Together, we possess the power to reshape our world, to bathe it in the glow of progress and sustainability.

Welcome to the Tribe. Welcome to a brighter tomorrow.

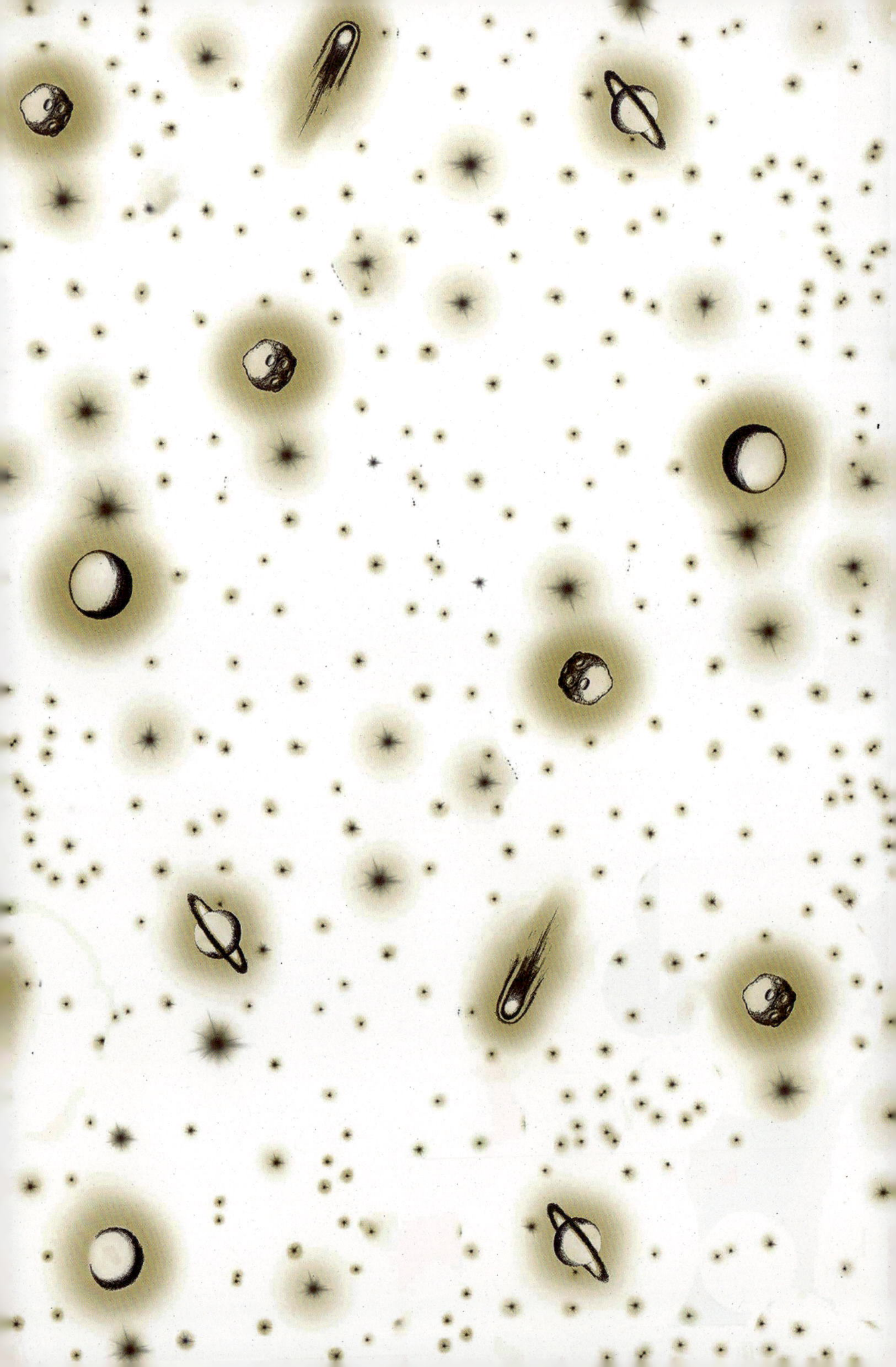

The Light Within Us

Xander Cadisch

[First Edition]

Phos Ltd
Unit 2, The IO Centre,
Hearle Way,
Hatfield,
Hertfordshire
AL10 9EW
UK

Ordering Information:

Quantity sales. Special discounts are available on quantity purchases by corporations, associations, and others. For details, contact the publisher at the address above.

Please contact Phos Ltd: Tel: +44 (0)20 8492 7633;
or visit www.phos.co.uk

Printed in the United Kingdom

ISBN 9-781399-973199

9 781399 973199

Thanks to Elaine, Dr Shelley, Professor Russell Foster, Karen, the Terrapin team, and every member of the Tribe who has got me here.

Xander Cadisch

The Light Within Us

Biophilic design, human behaviour, and the power of wavelengths

PHOS

Table of Contents

Table of Contents

Table of Contents

Table of Contents

Xander Cadisch

Xander holds the roles of Sustainability Director and Chief Technical Officer at Phos Ltd, a multi-award-winning lighting manufacturer with deep principles of biophilic design and a heritage going back to 1883. With a unique blend of qualifications – he is also a mixologist, distiller, and chef – Xander extends his expertise beyond the workplace, delivering lectures at universities throughout the UK about the power of light and organic design. His primary interest lies in exploring how sensory experience can enhance the overall quality of people's lives.

"We will never be truly healthy, satisfied, or fulfilled if we live apart and alienated from the environment from which we evolved."

Stephen R. Kellert

Foreword

Foreword by David Gilbey, Independent Architectural Lighting and Visual Designer; Lighting Design Director, Diriyah Gate Development Authority

They say that we all have a book in us - I feel that I have several! However, if I were to start writing one today, it would probably be a soft and fluffy tome on lighting projects around the world, full of anecdotes and inspiring stories. Although I am well versed in the psychology and neuroscience of light and how the eye receives light, I doubt that I would have committed to the long hours and commitment to research seen in this book at my very first attempt. In lighting, we all have a duty to research, to keep learning and to share our knowledge, especially with the young lighters of the future. Our degrees are a line in the past and we have to constantly feed the hungry design monkey inside us and keep replenishing our thirst for knowledge. I know the effort that has gone into this book, the many hours of research and conversations with experts in the field. I am going to read it; I am going to go back to it often and I am certain that I am going to learn from it.

There is an ill-considered hierarchy in design: designers consider themselves 'the experts', as they are to some degree, but we have to open our eyes and our hearts to ideas, knowledge and wisdom from wherever it comes. We do not always even know all the questions, let alone all the answers.

When I first heard that Xander from Phos was going to write a book on this subject, I was intrigued by the idea of a manufacturer stepping into what may be considered designers' territory. But who owns knowledge? Certainly not me - it is not exclusively owned. I spoke with Xander and was overwhelmed by his knowledge of the subject, his passion and his determination to reach a wider audience. The talk was inspiring, and I considered him a friend and equal from the start. The hierarchy with designers at the top is nonsense: worthy people are worthy people, talent is talent and a person should be measured on their character, vision and endeavours, not by their job title.

I am proud to have made a very small contribution to this book - and it is indeed tiny - Xander put all the effort in. To provide encouragement, benchmark some of the content and share my contacts for further discussion was the least that I could do for such a worthy cause. Communication takes place when the other person understands and I am certain that this book will play some small part in our understanding of this important topic. Personally, I love how the psychological can influence the physiological inside us, and how feeling better in ourselves can improve our physical wellbeing.

All credit goes to Xander for making the effort. I can only hope that, if I receive a copy, Xander has taken the trouble to sign my 'first edition'. I expect further great things from this man, and as his profile grows in our industry, one day I will look back and say 'I knew Xander when'.....

Preface

Smell and taste were, for the longest time, my favourite senses. Growing up, the flavours and scents of my family kitchen mesmerised me, and I became obsessed with how a good Sunday lunch could add so much value to my existence. From the age of five, I spent years cooking intensely at home, eventually becoming a competent chef. This was perhaps the start of my fascination with the senses and how they connect us to the world. It was undoubtedly the first time I realised I could nurture this connection to improve my quality of life.

When I turned 18, my tastes and focus quickly swung towards cocktails and late nights. A drink with my friends, like a Sunday lunch with my family, was a sensory experience to be crafted. Fortunately, my skills were easily transferred to liquid concoctions. I moved to Peru, launched a gin brand, and slung cocktails for the master distiller Sipsmith gin. However, the universe had other plans for me, and in 2017, my grandfather, father, and brother asked if I would join the family lighting company, Phos. This conversation was a profound turning point for me. I started noticing light everywhere I went; before I knew it, the principal focus in my life became sight.

The more I explored the subject, the more I realised how influential sight is for our existence and understanding of this world. Besides the severely visual impaired, sight is the main porthole to how we experience the world around us - a risotto may taste delicious, but if it looks like a dog's dinner, your other senses reel at the idea of shoving a spoonful of it in your mouth! And yet, as I started learning about the incredible lighting technologies that transform how our eyes engage with the world around us, I was surprised by the lack of education designers receive on light during their extensive years of studying. It seemed to me that we put more consideration into the zoos we build for animals than we do into the spaces we build for humans, and, as a result, we reduce the quality of our experiences in the spaces where we live and work. Vision is our primary means of interacting and connecting with the world around us, yet we hardly consider its impact on our well-being.

I speak from personal experience when I say that living in the fast-paced, artificial environment that we now call our habitat leads to medical issues and burnout. Our current systems are not working: we are damaging ourselves and the wildlife we share this planet with. But on a more optimistic note, as designers and consumers, we have the opportunity to truly shift the health of the world in the right direction. We simply need to live as nature intended. What we need to do is design naturally - to design biophilically.

What follows in this book is an amalgamation of eight years of reading, interviews and research that champions light in biophilic design, as well as the roles of lighting designers. We will examine how light has shaped and guided us through evolution and how to harness this for good. Also included are case studies from leading designers where these principles have been put into practice in a way that benefits all. Moreover, this book serves as a passionate homage to the pride I have for my family company and our commitment to making some of the world's finest biophilic luminaires.

Lighting technology has become available that offers us new and exciting ways to showcase and connect with our built spaces, and most of the world relies on artificial lighting in their homes and workspaces. However, the importance of artificial lighting is rarely considered in the context of the frameworks designers can use to create natural designs. Biophilic design is the means to ensure a sustainable, healing environment for human beings and nature to exist. This has to start with a deeper understanding of how and why we evolved to see what we do and how we connect with the world around us as a result. With this, we can arm ourselves with the knowledge of how best to design and illuminate the spaces we live in for the benefit of both people and the planet.

It must be noted that this content is designed to connect readers with what nature offers in the way of design. Designers can use principles that oppose aspects of design found in nature to create drama and focus in spaces (for example lighting galleries where high-contrast lighting can be used to focus viewers' attention on very specific areas in the space). It is extremely difficult to write one all-governing bible for design but this resource will certainly show you how to implement the factors of natural design that result in huge improvements in mental health and all-round improvements in performance.

I must give special thanks to Bill Browning, Catherine Ryan and Joe Clancy of the biophilic design outfit Terrapin, whose brilliant biophilic framework is the basis of this book's "how to" section. Additionally, Dr Shelley James has been a shining light in my journey into this world.

BUT FIRST - to get you enticed and to inspire you on the subject, scan the QR code to see the true power of light...

SCAN HERE

Overview

Section 1:

What is biophilic design?

Section 2:

How light shaped us – Eyes as windows to the world

Section 3:

How to : Terrapin's biophilic design principles

Section 4:

Case studies / Inspiration

Section 5:

Phos – Sustainable, biophilic lighting instruments

SECTION 1

What is biophilic design?

What is biophilic design?

The word "biophilia" was first introduced by psychoanalyst Erich Fromm, who defined it as the "passionate love of life and of all that is alive ... whether in a person, a plant, an idea, or a social group".[1] The term was later popularised by the biologist Edward Wilson, who suggested that our link with nature was inherited owing to our evolutionary dependence on it for survival and personal fulfilment.[2]

In 2008, Stephen Kellert, a professor of social ecology at Yale, popularised the notion,[3] and the use of the term "biophilic design" spread rapidly to the extent that it is now widely recognised and used within and outside the design community. However, a perception persists that it can be achieved simply by moving plants inside. This is not the case. Spaces can replicate functions in nature without containing a single plant (see below).

Figure 1 | Heathwick Studio, Cape Town. Natural, biophilic shapes creating awe and mystery amongst many other biophilic principles – and not a tree in sight! (Taken from Nature Inside by William D. Browning and Catherine O. Ryan, published by Terrapin).

Spaces containing not a single plant can replicate functions in nature.

When replicated correctly, the positive impact of biophilic design on human beings is immense. It can lower blood pressure, improve memory, lift mood and even increase healing rates in hospitals.[4] From a commercial standpoint, the use of biophilic design can both cut costs and drive growth and innovation. More generally, it can change the quality of an individual's life and their emotional connection to a space.

The constituent elements of biophilic design are experienced through our senses. When we see, hear, smell, feel, taste and move through the world around us, hormonal and neurological responses are triggered that can positively or negatively affect our basic levels of performance and contentment.[5] Our brains employ high-frequency brainwaves (gamma or beta waves) to perform tasks that require concentration and, afterwards, to restore stability to our ultradian rhythm (small biological cycles that occur during our daily circadian rhythm) we require a period of lower-frequency brainwave activity (alpha waves) which is generated by restorative cognitive activities.[6] Put simply, including environmental and biophilic features helps restore important natural rhythms, prompting physical, emotional, and cognitive responses through exposure to plants, animals, water, landscapes, and other natural elements.

When we lack visual contact with the natural world, for example when we are in a windowless and featureless space, many of us experience boredom, fatigue and, in extreme cases, physical and psychological abnormalities. Solitary confinement in prison is a psychologically and physically detrimental example of this.[4]

William Browning and Catherine Ryan, with the help of Joe Clancy - all experts in sustainable and environmental design - have conducted extensive research on how to optimise the design of spaces that we occupy. Their 15 principles of biophilic design (on which this book is primarily based) are the backbone of the now-famous Google office design, aimed at increasing the performance of all staff in their offices.[4] If Google are willing to spend millions of pounds to improve performance through natural design, surely we must all recognise the value it can bring.

Their overarching explanation of what is required for a design to be biophilic is given below. I break down their "how to" guide in Section 3.

1) A repeated and sustained engagement with nature.

2) A focus on human adaptation to the world over time.

3) Encouragement of emotional attachment to a space.

4) A way to connect people to nature so that relationships and responsibilities towards human and natural communities are encouraged and enhanced.

5) The encouragement of considered, integrated and connected architectural solutions.[4]

Benefits of biophilic design

The pandemic reminded us just how much we rely on our connection with nature. Huge numbers of us sought refuge in countryside homes[7] understanding that nature boosts our physical and emotional well-being.

Leading organisations have caught on to this, using this knowledge to improve the performance of human beings in the spaces we inhabit. By creating natural spaces that align with our evolution and physiology, we can nurture motivation and ability and ultimately, performance within the built environment.

In fact, a widely accepted formula for performance suggests that if someone is more able, motivated or has more of an opportunity, their overall performance will increase.

Figure 2 | Private residence, UK. Magic can be achieved through working vibrant, natural looking luminaries into biophilically designed spaces. Lighting consultant: Light House Designs.

The formula for this is shown below:

Performance = ability x motivation x opportunity

Modern measurement techniques objectively prove how natural lighting and spatial arrangements positively affect our bodies and minds.[8] Biophilic design, which mimics nature, has been proven to improve all three components of this performance formula and it is these that researchers, Terrapin, base their 15 principles of design upon in the "how to" section of this book.

Examples showcasing the benefits of performance-enhancing biophilic design, can be observed across every sector of the economy, as illustrated below:

Commercial

There is growing evidence that buildings are used strategically as sales and marketing tools,[9] and as employee "benefits" to attract and retain high-quality workers.[10] Becker and Lynn reported in 1986 that the ability to "wow" potential employees upon arrival at interview could help employers negotiate better salaries, recruit better staff and retain them for longer than if that wow factor was absent. They found that 40% of employees knew whether they would take the job by the time they arrived at reception:[10] first impressions do count.

Figure 3 | 73 Brook Street, Mayfair. Designers: Studio Indigo, Cheevers Howard, Clivedale, PLP Architecture.

"Productivity can triple under biophilic conditions[4]"

Desk jobs tie employees to their workstations for many hours a week, whether those hours are spent at home or in an office. Many studies have reported on various aspects of office environments that are required to make staff lives more comfortable:

• Subjects working in windowless rooms but who had plants worked more efficiently, had lower blood pressure readings, and felt more attentive than those working in the same room without plants;[11]

• Passive views of nature through looking out of windows, watching videos or looking at photographs have consistently been found to reduce stress and promote health, as have naturally designed areas;[12, 13]

• Nature-rich views help to restore cognitive capacity;[10]

• Access to daylight and natural views reduces the number of days that staff call in sick;[14]

• Workers who have views of nature from their windows feel less frustrated and more patient and report greater overall life satisfaction and better health than those who have no visual access to the outdoors or whose view is solely of built elements;[15]

• A study at the Sacramento Municipal Utility District in California showed that the cost of each workstation in the space was US$1,000. By repositioning the workstations so that employees had clear views of nature (instead of little to no view), employees' brains were able to shift into restoration mode (in which the eyes relaxed) and each employee increased their workload by 6% per hour, amounting to a return on investment of US$2,999 per workstation.[4]

Figure 4 | The Hilton, Park Lane. Lighting Designer: Elektra Lighting.

Healthcare

It is known that stressed bodies heal more slowly and are more prone to infection than relaxed bodies.[16] That may be why many studies show positive effects on health from adopting biophilia, which helps patients to relax.

• Patients recovering from gall bladder surgery recovered nearly 24 hours faster (8.5% faster) in biophilic rooms than those in nondescript, brick-walled rooms.[13]

• The typical stay in a US hospital is 4.8 days at the cost of US$4,221 per day. Across the 5,795 registered hospitals in the USA, this faster recovery time would amount to savings of US$89 million (£72 million) per year.[12] These patients also took fewer painkillers and called the nurses less often than those in non-biophilic rooms.[13]

Figure 5 | Thomas Pink, Jermyn Street | Designer: Not Limited

£72 million per year could be saved by making hospitals more biophilic

• Patients undergoing heart surgery who looked at images of nature before or after surgery had lower blood pressure and heart rate and improved recovery time than those who looked at blank paper.[17] Similarly, patients who looked at images of nature had lower blood pressure and heart rates and improved psychological traits when they were out in nature compared with patients in windowless spaces.[4]

• In Canada, patients who had undergone major heart surgery and who recuperated in rooms with good lighting had a mortality rate of 7%, compared with 12% among those in poorly lit rooms.[18]

• Babies in hospital who received 12 hours of sunlight and 12 hours of darkness in a 24-hour cycle were found to cry less and had better eye quality than those in poorly lit rooms.[18]

• In 1999, 12 care homes for the elderly in Amsterdam installed artificial light that mimicked the sun. Three and a half years later, their cognitive deterioration was significantly less than that among elderly people without the same type of light.[18]

• According to McLeod (2016), when London's Blackfriars Bridge was painted green, the suicide rate dropped dramatically.[19]

The positive effects of nature may extend to the immune system, directly affecting the human physical health.[13]

Retail

It is known that the longer customers spend in a space, the more likely they are to buy something. Traditional retail needs to focus on customer experience in the battle with online shopping[4] and many suggest a significant metric for retail brands would be measuring a customer's experience per square metre.[4]

Figure 6 | YOTEL hotel, Clerkenwell, London. Designer: Spaceagency.

Various studies have shown how natural design can boost customer experience and, in many cases, sales. For instance, Browning and Ryan (2020) reported that a well-ventilated store observed a 15-25% increase in the hedonic value of goods sold; sales were increased per unit area when daylight was brought into stores; the more trees on a shopping street, the higher the sales for stores that fronted onto the street; and living elements in window displays were found to increase the time that shoppers looked at the display.[4] In a specific example of the latter, aquariums in shop fronts were found to increase the time that shoppers spent looking at the display by 16%, and the number of people who stopped rose from 3.3% to 8.5%. Even shop employees' levels of happiness were found to improve when natural design principles were adopted, and these also improved the customers' experiences.[4]

Education

In schools, several projects have shown the advantages of the use of natural light and space.

- Creating natural islands of light was found to support concentration and cut noise levels by 6-8 decibels in classrooms.[20]

- Good quality light with no flicker has been found to improve the speed and accuracy of reading in schools.[20, 21]

- The rate of cognitive development over a school year was found to be increased in schools that had tree canopies on their grounds.[18]

- Exposure to natural spaces increased short-term memory performance by 14%.[4]

- Natural light in classrooms improved test scores by 7-8% and attention span by 13%.[21]

• Biophilic design was reported to promote positive association with school and therefore to increase levels of university attendance and general life outcomes.[4]

• Students seem to perform better under certain thermal and lighting conditions in a particular space.[20]

Hospitality

Biophilic changes in hotels can benefit hotel owners and customers alike. Customers prefer to have a view, so hotel managers charge around 18% more per night for a room overlooking water than they do for rooms without a view. A study on the interiors of hotels found that lobbies with biophilic traits were used 36% more than those without biophilic traits,[22] and this created a significant opportunity for hoteliers to increase sales of food and drink in lobbies. As customers, we tend to choose healthier foods and smaller portions in restaurants that have brighter, 'cool' lighting conditions than we do in dim, warm, 'cosy' settings.[23] Put simply, you can increase or decrease consumption based on lighting.

Residential

Our homes serve as the one constant sanctuary in our lives. Despite the stresses of work and the relentless stream of emails and messages, we return home to the same space and if we ensure that it fosters restoration, healing, and nourishment, we have a permanent betterment basecamp to regroup from. Unlike generic spaces like hotel lobbies, where design caters to a broad audience, our homes afford us the freedom to tailor biophilic features to our individual needs and preferences. They are the ultimate canvas for biophilic self-expression.

Biophilic design in our homes offers the same benefits shown in the examples spoken about previously. We feel this need to connect our homes to nature with objective metrics such as cash/cost. Studies show that properties situated on hillsides in Seattle with views of the lake command a 30% higher value compared to those without such vistas.[4] Similarly, lakeside homes enjoy a remarkable 127% premium.[4] These statistics underscore the tangible value of a connection with nature.

Ultimately, each of us can recognise the inherent worth associated with integrating natural elements into our living spaces. Investing in biophilic design not only enhances the aesthetic appeal of our homes but also ensures we can enrich our well-being and quality of life every day.

Figure 7 | The Newt Hotel, Somerset. Lighting Design: Illumination Works. Photography: Gavriil Papadiotis.

SECTION 2

How light shaped us –
Eyes as windows to the world

Figure 8 | The Big Bang. Cosmic ignition that created all the energy we feel and see.

How light shaped us – Eyes as windows to the world

The Savanna Principle asserts that the environment that moulded the human brain was drastically different from the world we currently live in.[1] We were once surrounded by irregular shapes, wide open areas, spaces with prospects and refuges, and vibrant, evenly distributed lighting conditions. We exist now in spaces adorned with materials that are made smooth and flat, light fixtures that are extremely limited in colour saturation, and wide-open office areas that offer little to no source of refuge. We are creating lower-quality spaces with lower-quality experiences. This, in turn, affects the health, wellbeing, productivity and enjoyment of people across the globe. So what does nature look like, and how do we experience the world around us?

To understand this, we need to look at the neuroscience of light, the visual system, and our evolution, which occurred outdoors over billions of years.

The evolution of sight

It all began with the Big Bang, around 13.7 billion years ago.[2] Every photon (packet of light energy) that tickles your retina comes from that moment in time. Every atom that makes up every retina and everything that the retina can see originated at the Big Bang. It quite beautifully connects the universe together.

Nearly all living organisms are dependent on the conversion of light energy to chemical energy by photosynthesis. The molecules that make land-based organic material are only possible because of photosynthesis; in this sense, we are all made of light. Moreover, as we will discover throughout this book, every fibre of our being, from red blood cells to our DNA, is influenced by light. It is the great constant of our planet's existence.

The origin of the first life on Earth is unknown, although it is thought to have formed around 3500 million years ago in the form of "cyanobacteria", also known as blue-green algae.[3] Over the next few million years, single-celled organisms became multicellular and bodies diversified into an array of invertebrates.[4]

While light was vital for photosynthesis and the first oxygen-breathing life forms, it was also key for survival, with visual systems developing to enforce night/day cycles, detect movement and make sense of the world around us.

The first step in the evolution of the human eye was the creation of light-sensitive cells at the base of a concave shape.[5] A few organisms still use this rudimentary system, but the exposure of these cells brought a risk of debris falling into them that could temporarily or even permanently blind the organism. Over time, the importance of this light-sensitive region led to mutations that caused the cells to become recessed deeper into the cavity, leaving only a small opening.[5] Eventually, a lens developed to protect the vulnerable opening, preventing twigs and other debris from restricting vision. Once the lens had developed, the ability to focus light to gauge distance became possible,[6] marking the appearance of the first 'eye' as we know it today.

When organisms moved from sea to land (for the largely uncontested food on drier pastures), they needed to retain the regular hydration that had served the eye up to this point.

Have you ever wondered why tears are salty?

They are a re-creation of the seawater that bathed the first primordial eyes and are a permanent, physical reminder of the connection to our earliest ancestors and the life they experienced.[7]

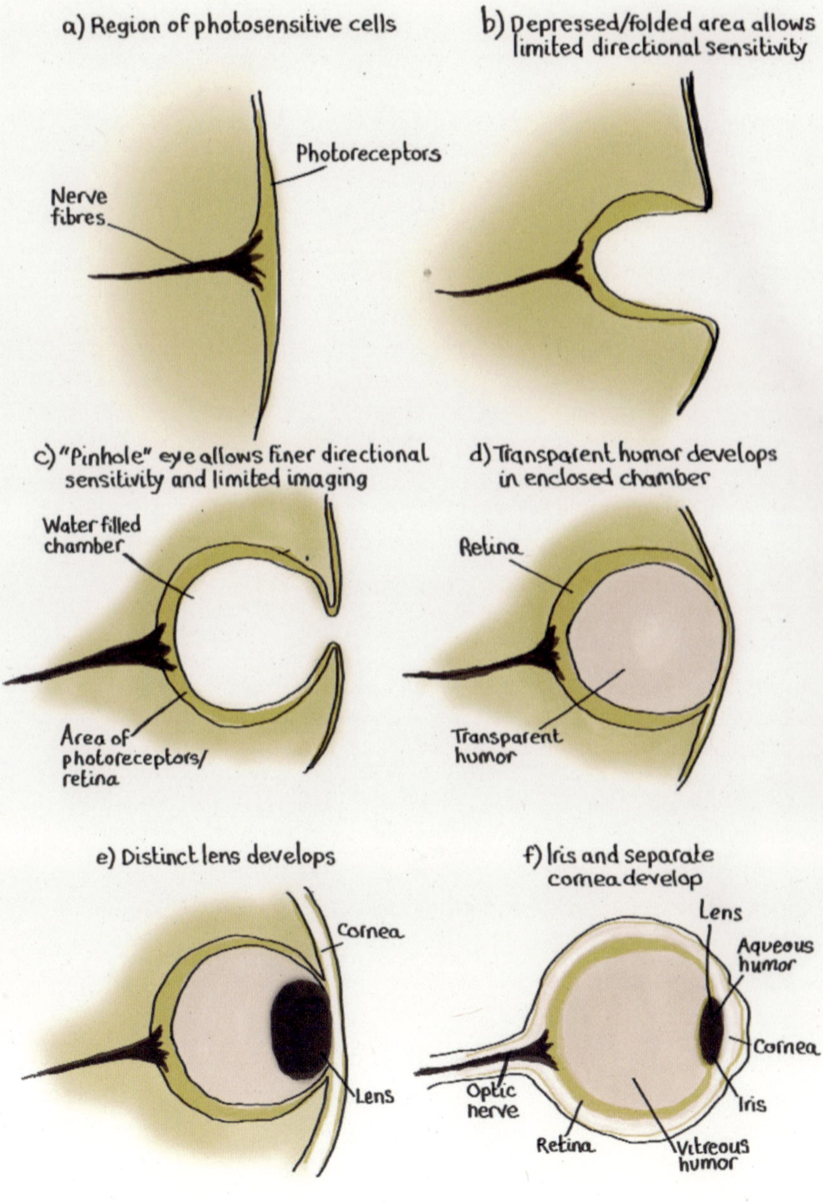

Figure 9 | Schematic diagram of the evolution of the human eye.

Figure 10 | Palaeontologists consider the Tiktaalik Roseae a classic example of an animal transitioning from life in water to that on land. Features of its skull, neck, ribs and appendages were shared with those of the earliest limbed animals (tetrapods), but it also had fishlike features such as scales and fin rays. It is thought to have lived in shallow water, propped up on its fins.

Tetrapods (land-living vertebrates that include humans) evolved from this stage to colonise dry land by developing limbs and the ability to breathe oxygen. They had skeletons able to stand strong without the support of water. Ribs and vertebrae changed shape and evolved to provide extra support and better distribute weight[8] while necks evolved to disconnect skulls from the rest of the body to allow better head mobility and absorb the shock of walking.[8] Bone formations shifted to create the five-digit pattern we see in our hands and feet.[9] Joints were developed to enhance movement and rotated forward to enable four-legged crawling.[8] Our hair thinned (we have as much hair as apes but ours is far thinner[10]) and, roughly 30 million years later, a body fit for walking on land, like the one we have today, evolved.[11] Each animal's visual system became specialised during this evolutionary journey. Human eyes evolved to decipher a thin section of the energy available in the world around us.

"The perfection of the eye as an optical instrument is a sign of just how important vision was in the struggle for survival"[10] and it is important to remember that, from an evolutionary perspective, apes are our common ancestor: we share 99% of our DNA with them. These apes evolved in the open air, and the expectations and understandings we have of the modern world derive from their evolution outside.

Insects have developed antennae; snakes have developed highly tuned tongues, while humans have developed retinas, described as "outgrowths of the brain".[12] These highly tuned instruments have over time enabled us to connect with the world around us, gathering visual information and optimising how we experience and understand the world. Like a plant leaning towards sunlight in a darkened room, they have budded out to connect with this valuable guide.

Figure 11 | Retina or antennae – outgrowths of the brain that are used to find visual information.

Our visual system relies on the white, "visible" spectrum of light. We can distinguish between 2 million and 7.5 million colours,[10] and each wavelength of colour has different effects. Red is arousing and causes an excited response;[13] blue activates the parasympathetic nervous system, which is the body's 'relaxation mode', and green flips between the two.[14] Not only do we use our colour vision to form ideas about the texture of objects in the world and what time of day it is, but we also use it to regulate our physiological state.

We often overlook the fact that colour is energy. However, when the visible light spectrum is framed in the context of the electromagnetic spectrum, we see that, "just beyond red is infrared, which we experience as heat, and just beyond violet is ultraviolet, which has been found to kill 'superbugs', like MRSA".[15]

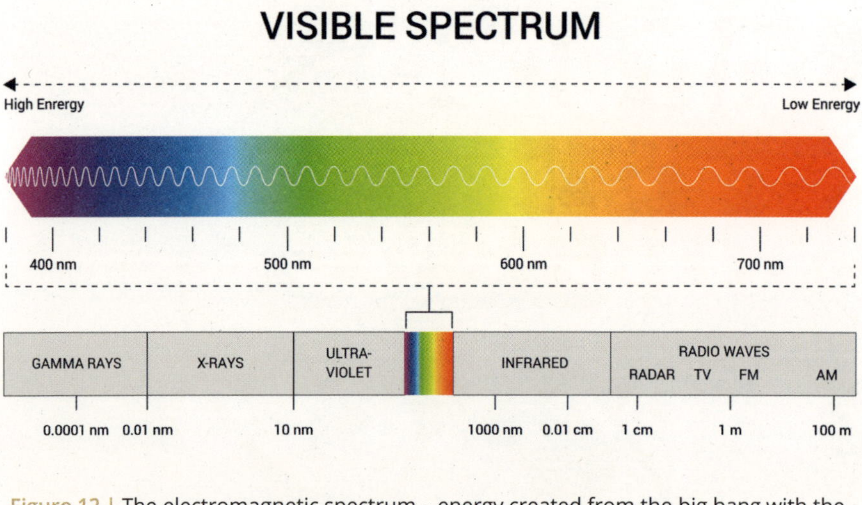

Figure 12 | The electromagnetic spectrum – energy created from the big bang with the visible spectrum being that which the human eye can detect.

"Just beyond red is infrared which we experience as heat[54]"

Light - Our haptic guide

The power of these wavelengths is clear when put in the context of the electromagnetic spectrum, but when we look deeper, we see that our visual system can add so much more to our experience of the world. Some of the earliest theories of sight, such as emission or extramission theory (300 BC), acknowledged that sight was linked to other senses. According to these theories, we reached out and 'touched' using invisible 'feelers' from our eyes, which enabled us to understand how objects felt, sounded, smelt and tasted.

In 1892, the term *haptik* was coined by the German psychologist Max Dessoir to describe a state of being able to 'touch' something acoustically or optically.[16] This was later embellished in Richard Gregory's top-down/black box theory (1970), which suggested that vision acts as a vessel in which we combine all previous experiences of our world, creating a deeper connection and understanding of everything around us.[17]

Gregory argued that we combine our past experiences of the world with each visual input to create an even richer understanding of the objects we observe.

For example, if we looked at the image shown in Figure 13 with no knowledge of smells, tastes, sounds or how things feel, the fruits would simply look like apples of varying shapes, colours and sizes. However, when we combine with this visual input the huge range of lived experiences that we all have, we quickly form an idea of how each apple would smell, feel and taste, and even the sound it would make if we dropped it from a height.

I hope that, by now, you are experiencing the same level of intrigue that I first felt when I looked deeper into light. It is an incredibly powerful influence on our bodies, with some suggesting that it accounts for up to 80% of how we interact with and make sense of the world.[18] With 100 billion signals sent to the brain every second,[10] light is a vessel on which all other senses can ride. An interesting phenomenon called "synaesthesia" shows the extent to which our senses are interlinked.

Figure 13 | Apples – more than meets the eye...

Synaesthesia - the combination of the five senses

Synaesthesia is a blending of the senses in individuals that commonly results in people 'hearing' colours, 'seeing' sounds or 'tasting' shapes. We all have synaesthesia to some extent...

Figure 14 | "Baluba" or "takete"? We give spiky objects 'spiky' names and tend to colour them according to their shape.

Psychologist Wolfgang Köhler first observed the "baluba/takete" effect in 1929.[19] He showed forms similar to those displayed in Figure 14 to a group of people in Tenerife and asked them which shape should be called "takete" and which should be called "baluba". The majority of the participants named the jagged shape "takete" and the rounded shape "baluba". The experiment has been widely repeated and the results are consistent.[20, 21, 22] It is unclear exactly why this pattern arises, but one theory is a synaesthetic connection; simply put, "baluba" sounds rounded and blobby, while "takete" sounds spiky. If participants were asked to assign colours to the shapes, they would probably assign a hot colour (such as red) to baluba and a cold one (perhaps yellow) to takete.[23]

We can all blend what we see with our other senses, so good quality lighting is essential in any space to ensure we gain the maximum sensory stimulation from what we see.

Texture and complexity are pleasurable

Browning and Ryan, in their book *Nature in the Space*,[24] explain how the human visual system initially receives wavelengths of light via rods and cones (named for their shapes) in a highly finessed system. The smallest receptor is two to three micrometres in diameter, roughly equivalent to two wavelengths of red light.[25] If the whole population of the USA stood on a postage stamp, they would be packed about as tightly as the rods are in a single retina.[25]

Figure 15 | The visual cortex. A funnel shaped part of the brain which deciphers objects. The more complex the object, the more pleasure is created.

After reaching the rods and cones, the light passes to the visual cortex. This funnel-shaped part of the brain is linked with many neurons (information sensors). The further down the funnel the information has to travel, the more neurons are stimulated, which means that more pleasure is created.[24] What this means, then, is that the more complicated an object is visually, the further down the funnel the signal goes and the more pleasure it creates! Think of the joy derived from a rustic wrought iron door handle compared to a "stick and slap" door handle from Amazon.

When we enter a human-made space, we first focus on living things (people and animals). Next, our eyes are drawn to interesting features in the room - decorative details and ornaments[24] - because we seek out things that look attractive. Yet because spaces in the modern world are often smooth and lacking in complexity, our pleasure is limited.

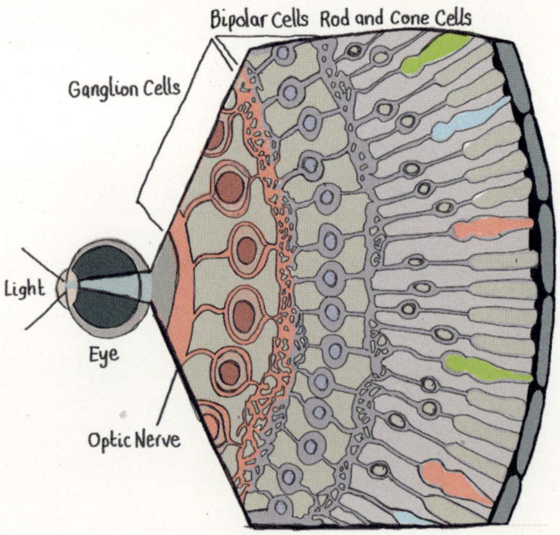

Figure 16 | Rods, cones and ganglion cells. Highly sensitive components of the human visual system.

Basic expectations of the natural world

Homo sapiens is distinguished by its large brain - and the species only developed that brain when it mastered fire.[26] The use of fire enabled us to cook our food, increasing calorie absorption significantly compared to raw ingredients. In hunter/gatherer times, this meant that less time was required for foraging and more time could be given to problem-solving and development of the logical/planning parts of the brain.[27] We would never have evolved into the creatures we are today on a raw-food diet (such as that of a gorilla) since we could never have consumed enough energy to support a larger brain.

Our brains process all our sensory inputs and at the start of our lives we operate using our hypothalamus, also known as the primal brainstem. This is responsible for our reactive connection to the world (our fight-or-flight response)[28] and allows simple reactions to circumstances around us, such as smiling, laughing or "throwing our toys out of the pram". When we reach adolescence, we rewire the primal brain to the frontal lobe, requiring huge amounts of sleep.[29] The frontal lobe is the part considered grown-up, primarily associated with planning and logical decision-making. We are quite literally rewiring ourselves to be more grown-up. The primal expectations still exist, however, so the more we can align with this simple part of the brain, the more pleasing we will find the space around us since we have inherited many of the expectations we have of the world through the learned experiences of our ancestors.

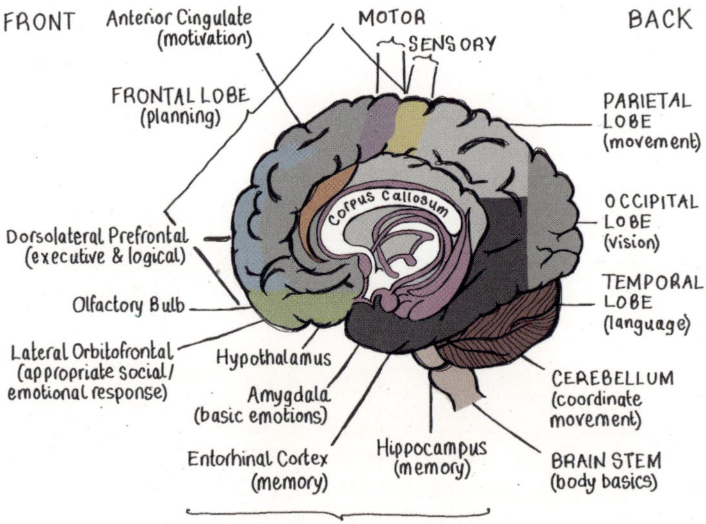

Figure 17 | Our primal brain (hypothalamus) and our modern brain (frontal lobe). The magic of fire gave us our modern perspective on things.

Experts have built a clear set of principles regarding what the brain "expects" to see in the world. Designers at companies such as Google, Microsoft and more widely, web and app developers, use these principles as a template to ensure that users of their products feel comfortable and calm. They are known as the "Gestalt principles of visual perception".

The seven Gestalt principles of visual perception

Max Wertheimer, Kurt Koffka and Wolfgang Köhler founded Gestalt psychology in the early 20th century.[30] The German word gestalt can be translated as "pattern" or "configuration," and Gestalt psychologists emphasise that the human brain is wired to see structure, logic and patterns.

1) The figure-ground principle

Figure 18 | A giant-sized bite or a projection with a person in the way?

The figure-ground principle states that people instinctively perceive objects as being either in the foreground or the background. They either stand out prominently in the front (the figure) or recede into the back (the ground). In the image above, our brain can easily understand that the person is in front of the apple.

2) Similarity

Figure 19 | A few seconds of looking at the image leads us to group similar shapes.

The principle of similarity states that when things appear to be similar, we group them. We also tend to think similar objects have the same function. At first glance, the shapes in the image shown in Figure 19 appear to be placed randomly, but we soon see that the circles are grouped and understand that the triangles are part of a separate entity that surrounds the main shape formed by the circles in the centre.

"We have inherited many of the expectations we have of the world through the learned experiences of our ancestors."

3) Proximity

Figure 20 | Together or apart? We see the image on the left as one unit and that on the right as two, even though the circles are the same in both.

The principle of proximity states that objects that are close together appear more related than those spaced further apart. In Figure 20, we see the image on the left as one cohesive unit, while that on the right contains two separate units.

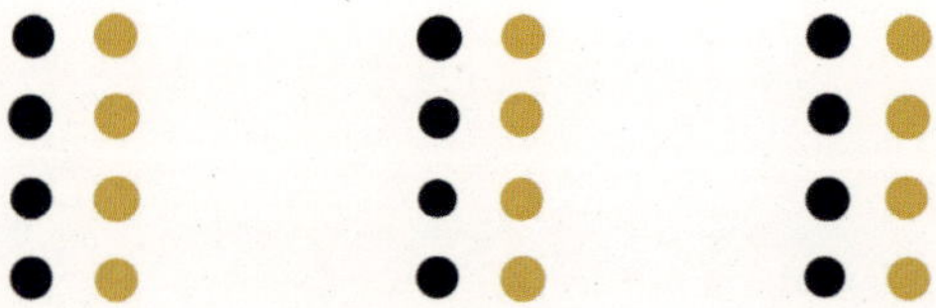

Figure 21 | Proximity is paramount: first we see three groups of eight dots, then we see the colour pattern.

Figure 21 illustrates how the relative nearness of objects has a stronger influence than colour on grouping. Proximity is so powerful that it overrides any similarity of colour, shape or other factors that may differentiate a group of objects.

4) Common region

The principle of the common region is related to proximity. When objects are located within the same closed region, we perceive them as being grouped (Figure 22). The addition of borders or other visible barriers creates a perceived separation between groups of objects, even if they have the same proximity, shape, colour, etc.

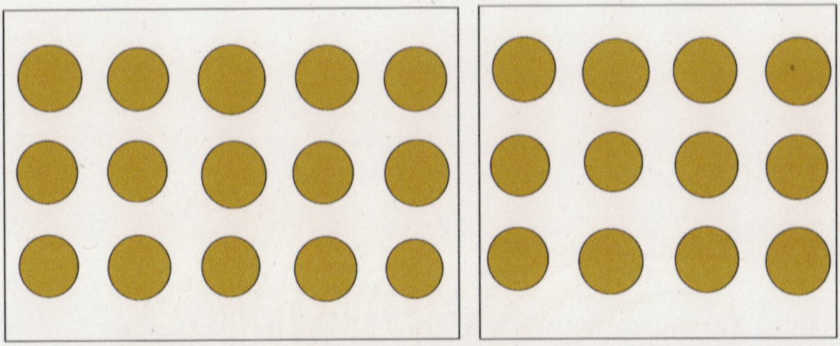

Figure 22 | A box of five columns and a box of four: the placement of borders around these circles leads us to see two units even though the nine columns of circles are the same distance apart.

5) Continuity

The principle of continuity explains that objects arranged on a line or curve are more closely related than elements that are not on the line or curve.

In Figure 23, we sense that the gold dots in the curved line continue into the black dots and the black dots from the left form a straight line since the eye naturally follows the curve and line. Hence, continuation is a stronger signal of relatedness than colour.

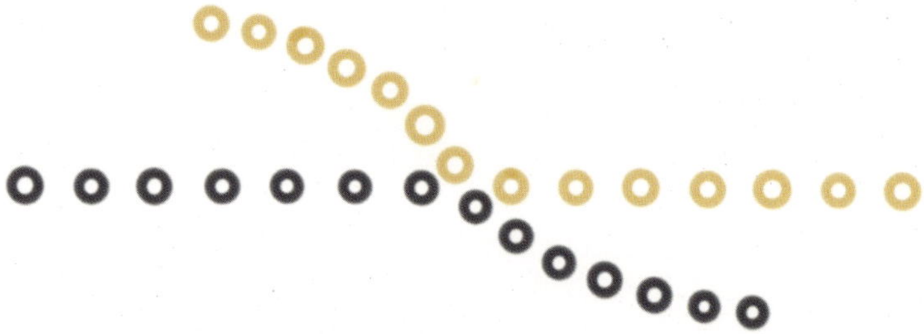

Figure 23 | A straight line and a squiggle? An illustration of how shape is more prominent than colour.

6) Closure

Figure 24 | Black and white lines or a recognisable animal? We seek a pattern to such an extent that we don't notice some parts are missing.

The principle of closure states that when we look at a complex arrangement of visual elements, we seek a single, recognisable pattern. When we see an image that has missing parts, our brains fill in the blanks to make a complete and recognisable picture. The image shown in Figure 24 is seemingly black and white lines, but we connect these to create a coherent shape in the form of a zebra.

7) Focal point

The focal point principle concerns the place to which the attention is first drawn. When we look at the image in Figure 25, we first notice the gold square because it is different from all the black circles around it. The first point of interest grabs our attention; from there, our focus moves to other parts of the image.

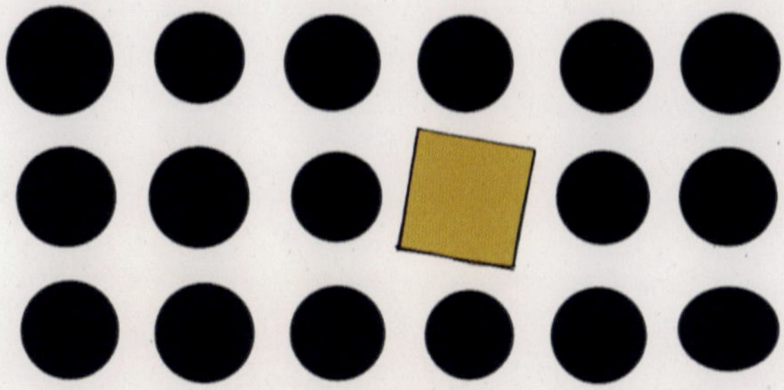

Figure 25 | Less is more – one gold square grabs the attention in a sea of black circles.

Space and place - "what" and "where" objects are

When we look at an object, our perception of it begins when the eye, in which the pupil has adapted to the intensity of the light, focuses the light onto the retina, where it is absorbed by a layer of photoreceptor cells.[31] These cells, comprising rods and cones, convert the light into electrochemical signals. Rod cells are responsible for our night vision and respond well to dim light. Rods are found mainly on the edges of the retina, so most people will find that they can see better at night if they focus their gaze just to the side of whatever they wish to observe.[32]

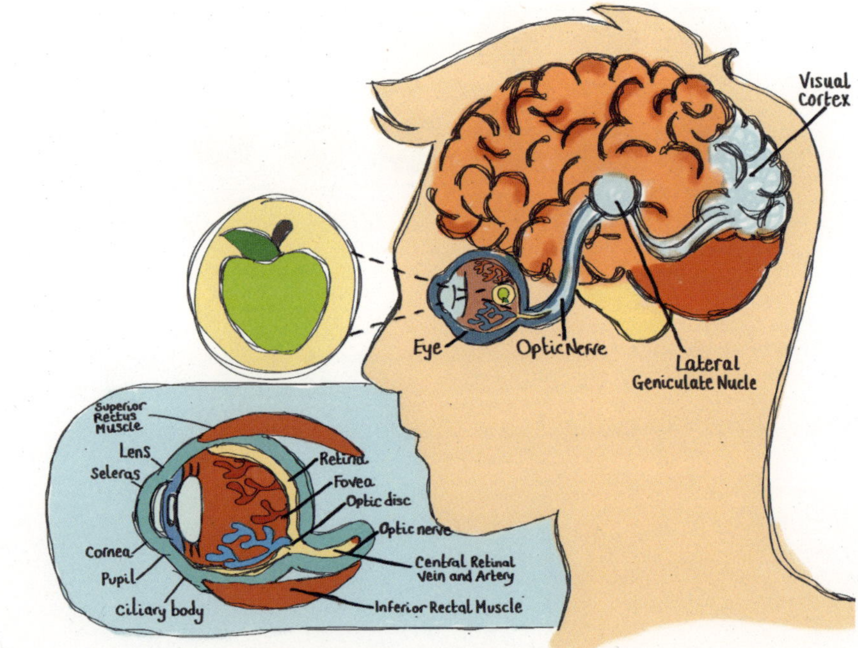

Figure 26 | Faster than the blink of an eye: information is passed from the retina to the visual cortex almost instantaneously.

Cone cells are concentrated in a central region of the retina called the fovea; they are responsible for high-acuity tasks such as reading and colour vision. Cones can be subcategorised into three types, depending on how they respond to red, green and blue light. In combination, these three cone types enable us to perceive colour.[33]

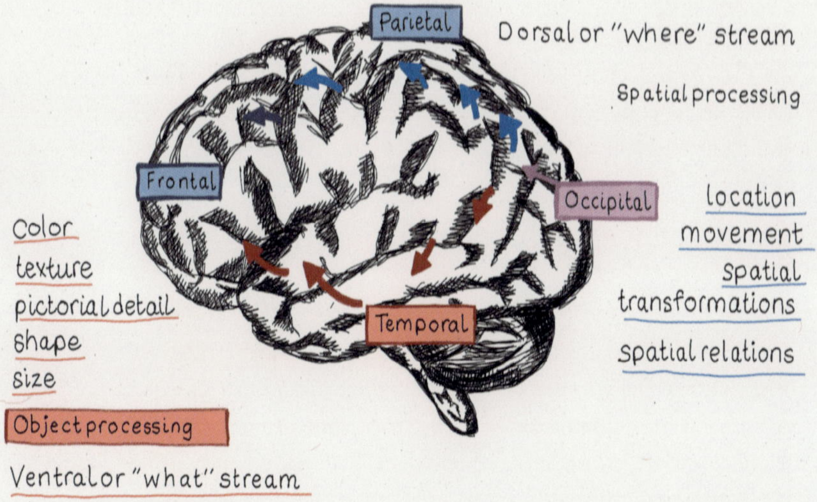

Figure 27 | The ventral and dorsal pathways work out "what" and "where" objects are.

A key part of the brain known as the superior colliculus is responsible for moving the eyes in short jumps, called saccades. Saccades stitch together a series of relatively still images to enable the brain to perceive the whole picture as a smooth scan.[33] Saccadic eye movement solves the problem of extreme blurring that would result if the eyes could pan smoothly across a visual landscape. They can be readily observed if you watch someone's eyes as they attempt to pan their gaze across a room.[33]

About 130 million photoreceptors absorb the light, and roughly 1.2 million axons (part of the neurons) of ganglion cells transmit information from the retina to the visual cortex, which lies in the occipital lobe of the brain.[34] This happens incredibly fast. A 2006 University of Pennsylvania study calculated the approximate bandwidth of human retinas to be around 8960 kilobits per second. For comparison, guinea pig retinas transfer at a rate of only around 875 kilobits per second[34] - we have a highly tuned piece of sensory equipment! The passage of the signals through the photoreceptor and ganglion cell layers enables us to detect contrast changes within an image (such as edges or shadows).[35] The visual information regarding the object we see is deciphered after it exits the occipital lobe and follows two main pathways or streams:

In the ventral stream (the "what pathway") the object is visually identified and recognised. The dorsal stream (the "where pathway") processes an object's location relative to the viewer.[36]

The more natural the images and shapes, the smoother our visual processing of the environment.[24] With smoother visual processing comes greater calm and contentment.[37] However, the more uniform the object, the fewer the wavelengths that are sent to the retina; and when these wavelengths are tuned down in this way, so too is the brain's ability to tell what and where an object is.

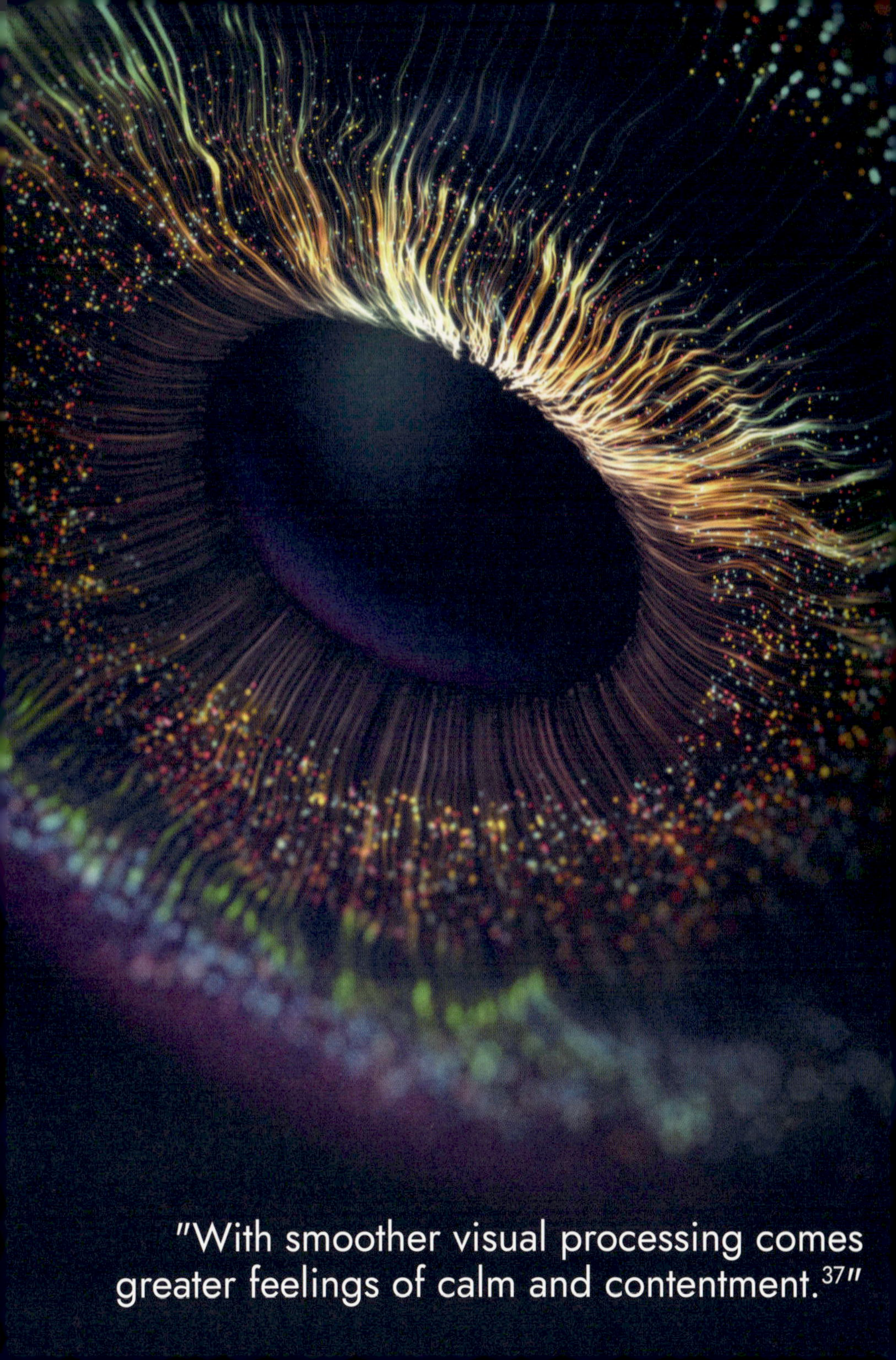

"With smoother visual processing comes greater feelings of calm and contentment.[37]"

Fractals

Nature is characterised by a particular type of statistical geometry known as fractal geometry.[38] Humans evolved in complex and sensory-rich natural environments that were defined by fractals on both large and microscopic scales.[39] In nature, fractal shapes can be observed in everything from the humble fern to the structure of the universe. Currently, most of the global population lives in built urban environments characterised by straight lines, right angles, empty planes, rectangles, cubes and cylinders, resulting in spaces that do not adequately nurture and revitalise. Abundant research in environmental psychology suggests that humans need the fractal scales, rich patterning, spatial layering and interlocking geometries that are typical of nature.

By removing this complexity, we risk transforming our vibrant world–a tapestry of colours, shapes, and textures that invigorate and inspire–into a barren landscape devoid of heart and soul. We should celebrate the beauty of imperfection. It is the true essence of nature.

The four fractal groups

It is hard to define fractals precisely, although most are linked through the exhibition of four common fractal features:

- Infinite intricacy
- Zoom symmetry
- Complexity from simplicity
- Fractional dimensions

These are explained overleaf.

Figure 28 | Fractals. A series of repeating patterns, at many different scales, where any small part resembles the whole.

Figure 29 | Kaleidoscope of Rubjerg Knude lighthouse by RPHFOTO.

1) Infinite intricacy

Karl Weierstrass discovered the first fractal shape. He drew an extremely jagged zigzag and found that it revealed more and more corner points and no smoothness the further the viewer zoomed.[39]

2) Zoom symmetry

Benoît Mandelbröt discovered that, if a viewer zooms in on a small fractal region, they are still looking at the same shape they started from.[40] Tiny bits of the fractal look the same as the whole.

3) Complexity from simplicity

Figure 30 | A fern by mathematical formula.

The influential 1988 book *Fractals Everywhere*[41] by Professor Michael Barnsley explained an algorithm known as the chaos game, which allowed computers to generate rapidly any fractal shape from its known mappings.

The image in Figure 30 shows one result of the use of this algorithm. It is not a real fern, but a mathematical image generated by playing the chaos game with the use of four particular maps. These complex natural shapes were encoded through the application of fractal geometry that used simple mathematical rules; in other words, complex shapes exist in nature as a result of the application of simple mathematical rules.

4) Fractional dimensions

The last and most striking feature of fractals is that they are not one, two- or three-dimensional, but somewhere in between. They exist in 3D, and the make-up of an object is predictable and organised as it grows in volume.[41]

Figure 31 | Saturn's rings are natural phenomena that follow mathematical rules.

Physiological responses to light and colour

Circadian rhythms

Circadian rhythms are the names given to nature's biological clocks (from the Latin *circa* (about) and *dies* (day)).[42] They influence everything from how sunflowers track the sun from east to west, to the timing of the monarch butterfly's migration, to the morning peak in the number of cardiac arrests in humans.[43]

Light is the main cue driving the human body's biological clock, and the timing of awareness of light affects many bodily functions including the release of hormones, sleep-wake cycles, metabolism, cell growth, cell proliferation and DNA repair.[44]

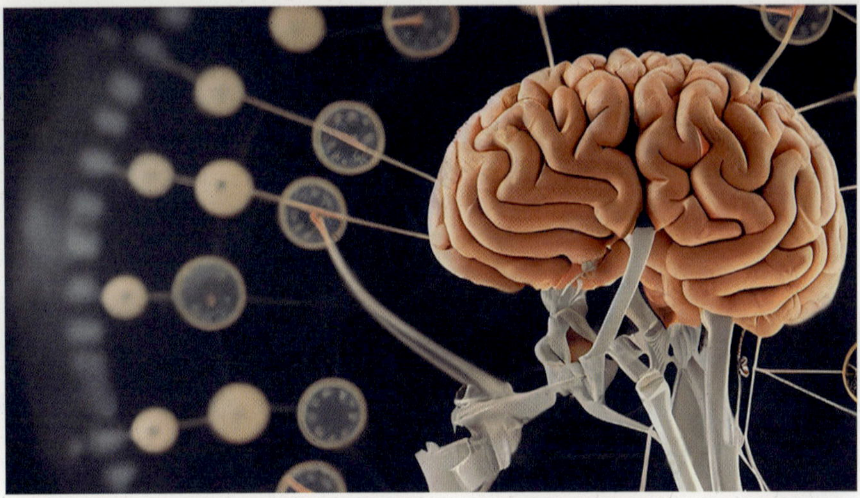

Figure 32 | Circadian rhythms – the body's clock and our main way of synchronising with the world around us. Generative AI by Jonatan.

"Light is the main cue for the human body's biological clock[44]"

In the early 1990s, Professor Russell Foster was ridiculed by scientists for showing that animals with no functional rods and cones (the two types of photoreceptor in the human retina) in their eyes were able to shift the timing of their circadian rhythms in response to a light pulse. Vision scientists refused to accept that, for 100 years, they had missed a class of photoreceptors in the eye that was responsible for this ability. In 2002, Brown University scientist David Berson found the last piece of the puzzle: a new class of photoreceptors - the intrinsic photo retinal ganglion cells (IPRGCs).[44]

**Scan to view
Russell Foster video**

So, what are these cells? While their name seems lengthy and complex, their function is simple: to keep the biological body clock synchronised with the natural timing of the outside world.[46] IPRGCs enable us to anticipate predictable events in our environment and to fine-tune our physiology to optimise our behaviour in response to a circadian rhythm.

IPRGCs are found in the retina. They respond to light through a light-sensitive protein they contain called melanopsin. This responds to blue wavelengths (around 480 nanometres on the electromagnetic scale[47]) to signal to the body what time of day it is.

One of the principal parts of the brain affected by signals from IPRGCs is the suprachiasmatic nucleus (SCN), a pea-sized area right at the base of the primal brainstem. Like an orchestral conductor, the SCN synchronises all the natural cues that set the body's circadian rhythms. These include the times of day at which we exercise, eat breakfast and dinner, and the period between sunrise and sunset. This extraordinary circadian network defines our co-existence with the world around us. Of all the circadian cues, light has the most effect.[48]

We evolved in the natural world and our body clocks were aligned with the rising and setting of the sun.[49] As the sun rose above the horizon, the sky glowed, and blue wavelengths cascaded through the atmosphere into our eyes, prompting our bodies to produce cortisol, the body's stress hormone.[49] Heart rates increased, blood pressures rose, and like an engine starting up for the day, our bodies fired into action.

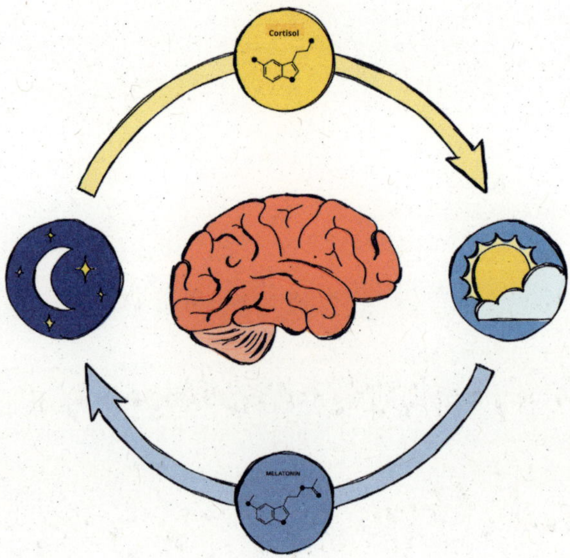

Figure 33 | The brain using melatonin and cortisol to guide us in day/night cycles.

However, that morning experience is extremely different in the modern world. Some of us wake up, have a coffee and begin work without seeing natural light. (It has been reported that adults spend on average just one hour a day outside, which is less than the United Nations' legal requirement for prisoners![50]) Natural light is around 50-100 times brighter than the lighting environment of homes and offices in the morning and typically around 5,000-10,000 times brighter by noon.[50] If we travel by public transport or in a car from home to the office or sit at our home workstations all morning, we are not receiving sufficient blue light to trigger our bodies' wake up responses. Moreover, without blue light, we do not counter the production of melatonin, the hormone that causes us to build sleep pressure and rest/repair.[51]

To illustrate just how powerful this light-sensing operation is, a blast of bright, blue-peak light has been found to increase alertness and focus by the same amount as 240mg of caffeine - equivalent to a double espresso - and it beats coffee when it comes to improved accuracy.[53] If we wake up and activate cortisol production by using blue light, we halt the production of our sleep hormone and tell our bodies it's time for action. When we have a coffee a few hours later, there is no sleepiness to battle with, and we'll be firing all day!

Conversely, if we receive this injection of blue light in the evening when we should be winding down and repairing (through the use of melatonin), the biological consequences can be huge. A study of 3,000 people in France showed that shift workers who worked at night for 10 years had lower memory and cognitive scores than those who worked during the day.[54] As Provencio and Foster put it, "Our headlong rush into modernity, without a second thought to our biology, is having a profound impact on our health."[45]

Light and health

Light acts as the 'winder' on our biomechanical watch.[55] If we go against deeply engrained biological expectations, we risk serious ill-health: IPRGC stimulation at the wrong time of day causes individuals to override the natural drive towards sleep and activates a stress response instead. Sustained activation of the stress response is associated with a range of health problems, from metabolic abnormalities such as diabetes to cardiovascular problems, high blood pressure and even immune system suppression. As mentioned previously, night-shift work (in which workers are exposed to high doses of blue light generated by LEDs) can be extremly problematic. In fact, it is now classified as "probably carcinogenic" by the World Health Organisation (WHO).[54]

On a more positive note, regulating the circadian rhythm and sleep/wake cycle can have a therapeutic effect. In 2013, Dan Freeman, Professor of Clinical Psychology at the University of Oxford, was able partially to stabilise sleep in schizophrenic patients and to reduce their levels of measurable paranoia by 50% by regulating their sleep.[46] According to Professor Foster, sleep "is our most important cognitive enhancer. When we sleep, we are coming up with new ideas, innovative solutions to the complex problems we face today."[42]

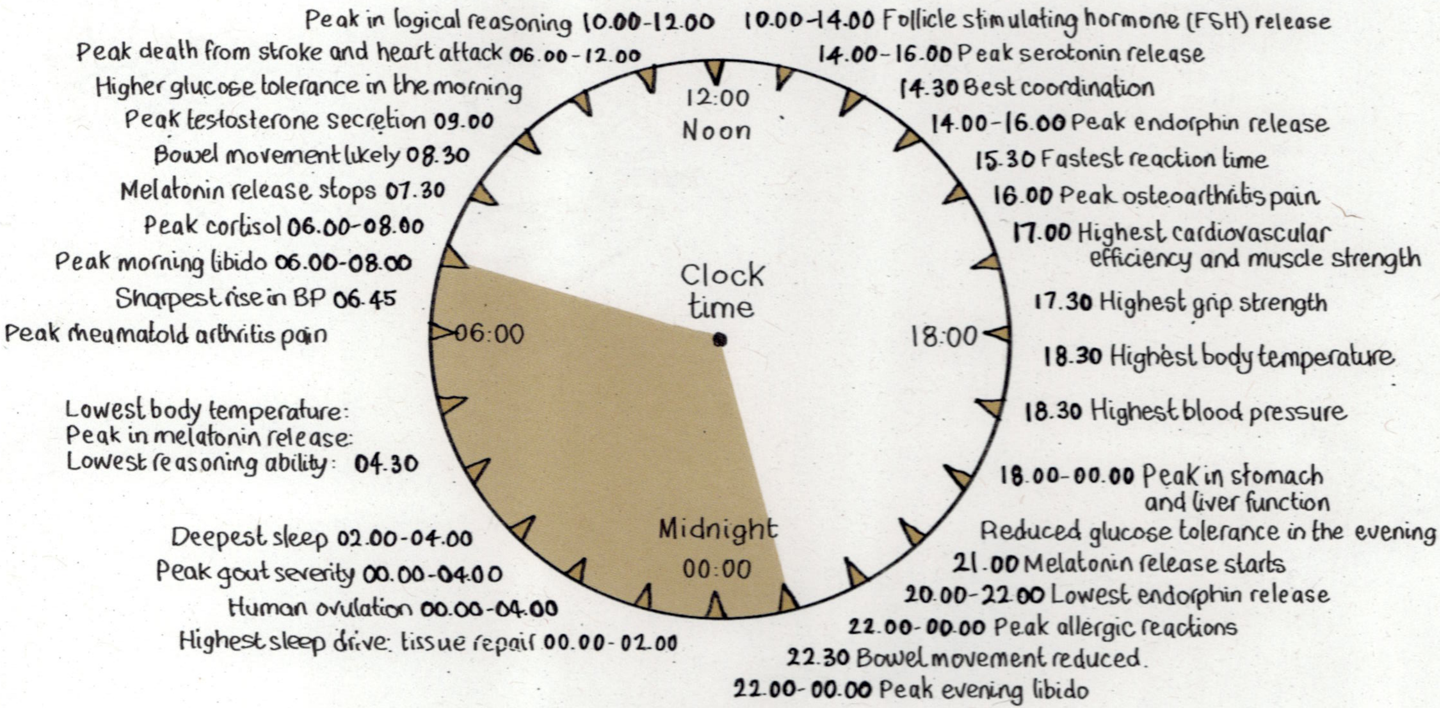

Figure 34 | Russell Foster's chart of circadian rhythms and their effects. Taken from Foster, R.G. (2020). Sleep, Circadian Rhythms and Health.[43]

• Over half of WHO essential medicines target molecular pathways that rely on internal clocks.[56]

• In 1896, a scientist called Niels Finsen healed 86% of his tuberculosis patients by using light (blue, violet, and ultraviolet).[56]

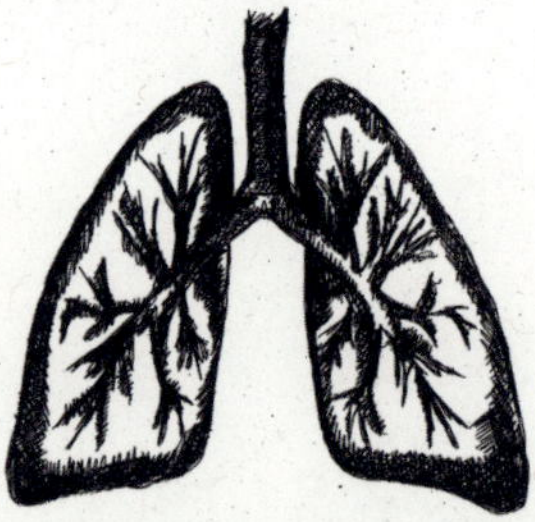

• Multiple sclerosis is three times more common in people who had low vitamin D levels as children.[56]

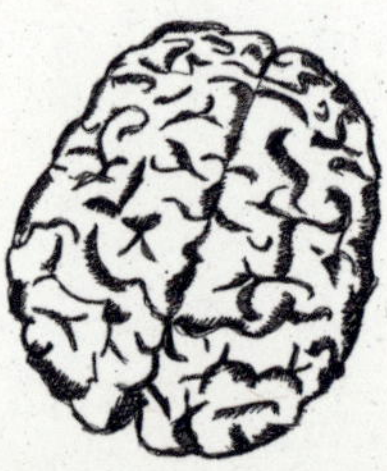

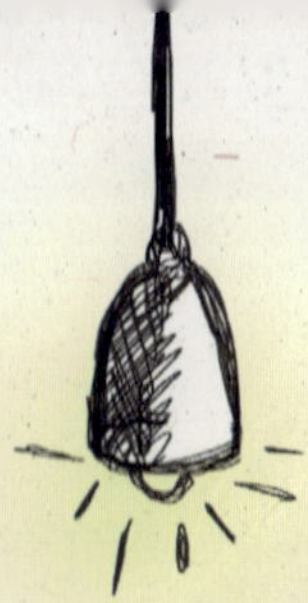

To show just how much our bodies change throughout the day, and consequently, how much these signals can affect them, I list some of my favourite facts below:

- Francis Levy studied the times at which people took prescribed drugs and how the time of ingestion altered their effects. Oxaliplatin, which is deemed an extremely potent bowel cancer medicine (and can result in nausea, vomiting and numbness/burning), worked far more effectively at certain times of day and one patient had no side effects, believing that they had been given a placebo.[55]

- In 1999, 12 care homes for the elderly in Amsterdam collaborated to use bright light fixtures between 10 am and 6 pm each day. After 3.5 years, it was found that their cognitive deterioration had significantly reduced from the levels observed before the lights were fitted. The use of melatonin and bright light helped them to function far more effectively and use fewer sleeping pills.[56]

"Every fibre of our being, from red blood cells to our DNA, is influenced by light.[46]"

"Blue-peak light has been found to increase alertness and focus by the same amount as 240mg of caffeine – equivalent to a double espresso...[53]"

• Most world records have been set in the early evening.[56]

• Swimmers swim the fastest and cyclists have the least exhaustion in the evening.[42]

• Football, tennis, and badminton skills peak in the early afternoon.[43]

• Tennis serves are more accurate in the morning but faster in the evening.[43]

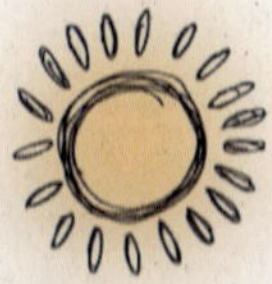

- Morning inoculations against flu are more effective than afternoon inoculations in generating an antibody response.[57]

- Taking anti-hypertension medication at bedtime almost halves the number of cardiovascular deaths compared with morning dosing.[58, 59]

- Radiation therapy for cancer results in significantly more hair loss if given in the morning rather than the afternoon.[60]

- Muscle strength, reaction time, flexibility and speed all peak in the late afternoon and early evening.[61]

All light – not just sunlight – contributes to circadian photo-entrainment. Given that we spend much of our waking day indoors, insufficient illumination or inappropriate lighting design can cause circadian phases to drift, especially if combined with inappropriate light exposure at night. Humans are constantly sensitive to light and, under normal circumstances, light exposure in the late night/early morning will shift our rhythms forward (a phase advance), whereas exposure in the late afternoon/early night will shift our rhythms backwards (a phase delay). To maintain optimal, correctly synchronised circadian rhythms, the body requires periods of brightness and darkness.[42]

Chronotypes

Within the general human circadian cycle, each individual has their own body clock or "chronotype".[62] Our tribal ancestry required that at least one tribe member would "keep watch" at all times of day,[63] so we developed in a way that ensured that each tribe member followed a unique waking and sleeping pattern. This way, there was a high chance that at least one member of the tribe was awake to protect and warn of danger.

In the modern world, most of us do not align with our chronotypes (except for those in the German town of Bad Kissingen, which has become the first "chronotype" town).[56] As a result, 69% of people suffer from "social jet-lag" each week[56] as they are forced to wake up earlier than their body clock intends. For every hour of social jet-lag per week, the likelihood of being overweight increases by one-third, and the risk of cardiovascular illness increases by 11%. You will be fatter, grumpier and sicker.[56] About 20% of accidents on the UK's roads are sleep-related,[56] suggesting that pressure on health services could be alleviated and many lives saved if we aligned with our biology. Moreover, from an educational perspective, asking a teenager to get up at 7 am is the equivalent of asking a 50-year-old to get up at 5 am.

Teenagers need nine hours of sleep but get 6.5 on average.[42] Imagine a world in which we arrived at work or school healthy, happy and hungry for success, instead of stumbling in unwell and drowsy to face a day of serious challenges. If our buildings dissolved the barrier between inside and outside so that we could connect our body clocks to the natural rhythms of the sun outside, we would be happier, more efficient and more connected to the world in which we live.

After this somewhat "downer" of a paragraph, let us see which chronotype you are...**Bear, dolphin, lion or wolf.**

Figure 35 | The four chronotype groups that most humans are members of. Which one are you?

Clinical psychologist Dr Michael Breus describes four chronotypes based on the sleep-wake patterns seen in animals.[64] Answering his online chronotype quiz will identify whether you are more of a bear, wolf, lion or dolphin. Figure 35 shows the principal characteristics of each.

Colour and communication

A major factor in our survival and development is our ability to form strong social bonds. There is significant evidence of just how important this is when we look at the visual development of infants.

Figure 36 | Development of the human visual system with red being the first colour we develop – vital for communication.

During the first days of life, babies see in black, white and shades of grey, and respond only to high-contrast outlines of faces.[65] The first colour they are able to perceive is at the red end of the spectrum. Scientists speculate that this is due to a deep primal need to recognise facial expressions and choose ripe food. Recent research supports these theories, as changes in blood flow to different parts of the face are reliable signals of a change in facial expression even in the absence of other cues, such as the shape of the eyes and mouth.[66] Figure 37 is a study showing the ability of individuals to determine mood simply by looking at pixellated images of varying blood flows in a subject's face. We are accurately able to predict emotions based on these vague images of red.

So, how is this relevant in the scheme of biophilic design? Well, the way in which we we light our spaces has evolved dramatically. We now use LEDs as the primary illumination source, and their effect on every aspect discussed above is both terrifying and inspiring.

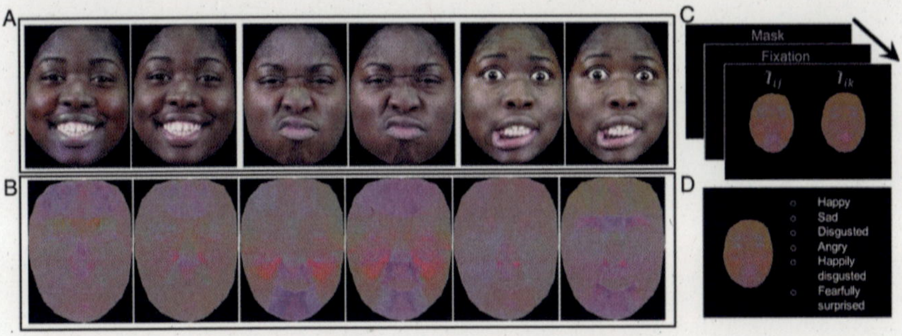

Figure 37 | Facial colour is an efficient mechanism to visually transmit emotion - Scientific Figure on ResearchGate.

Available from:https://www.researchgate.net/figure/A-The-first-pair-of-imagescorresponds-to-the-expression-of-happiness-the-second-pair_fig2_32386

The modern light source – the LED

An LED is a semiconductor light source that emits light when a current flows through it. LEDs offer many advantages over incandescent light sources, including lower power consumption, longer lifetime, improved physical robustness, smaller size and faster switching.[67]

Early LEDs emitted a red wavelength. These devices were not efficient enough for practical commercial applications, but the creation of a high-bright blue LED in 1993, by Japanese-American engineer and Nobel prize-winner Shuji Nakamura, changed the picture entirely.

These blue LEDs did not replicate the natural "white" light in which humans evolved. Around 2014, the blue wavelengths were combined with different phosphor coatings to produce green and red light through fluorescence. These, when blended, gave the appearance of white light, effectively raising the colour-rendering index (CRI) - a measurement of how well artificial light replicates natural light. When we look at light using a spectrometer, however, it is clear that these LEDs are far from what we consider to be natural light. Figure 38 shows the true makeup of sunlight vs various forms of LED chips.

Our circadian rhythms (and consequently our health) are adversely affected by poor quality lighting, as is our ability to see everything around us clearly, including the expressions on the faces of our loved ones (since red is not present in entry-level LEDs and blood flow requires a red wavelength for us to see it). The introduction of ill-considered light sources into the spaces we design has many effects.

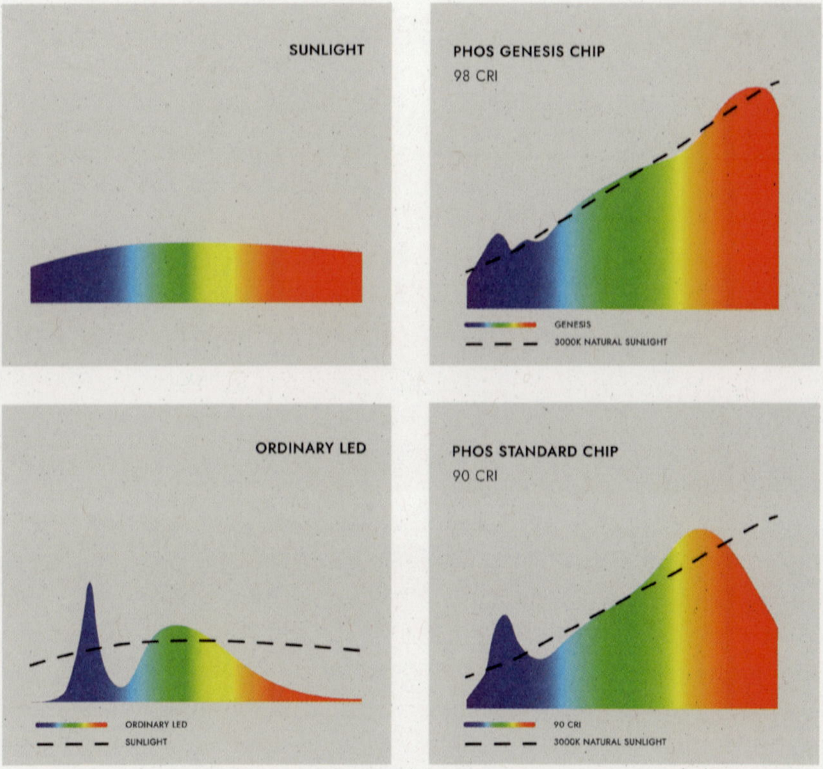

Figure 38 | The quality of natural sunlight vs various industry LEDs. Vast amounts of colour are lost when poor artificial lights are used in the built environment. This dramatically reduces the energy that bounces around the space.

Impact of poor lighting

Clever use of colour can change how we experience a space. We can make it cosy, bright, calm, stressful, focused, or romantic by triggering different autonomic responses and invoking our limbic brain. A holistic understanding of the range of information we process through our visual system and how our bodies respond can make our design choices more ergonomic and help us feel more in touch with the spaces we live in. However, if we use light sources that have little or no colour and build them into a space in a way that feels unnatural, we reduce dramatically the emotional experience that we can tap into within a space (since there are fewer energetic wavelengths bouncing around that we can connect with).

The way colours interact with each other plays a crucial role in shaping our emotional responses. Karen Haller puts it nicely, saying one can "picture wavelengths as ocean waves - sometimes short and frequent, other times tall and spread out. Each colour corresponds to a specific wavelength and frequency, contributing to the rich tapestry of light we perceive."[15] Research delving into the intersection of colour and psychology suggests that colour affects how we think, feel and behave. In essence, different wavelengths of light elicit different emotional responses from us.

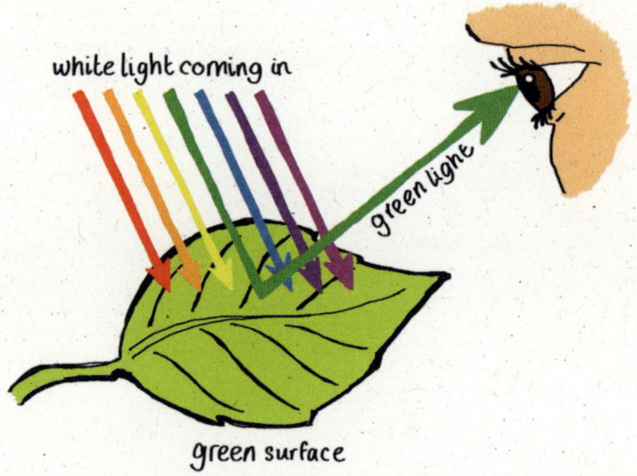

Figure 39 | Light sources containing a wide range of wavelengths will make spaces appear more colourful and vibrant. Objects can only reflect colours if they are there in the first place.

Consider the colour known as "Baker-Miller Pink", a colour reputed to "reduce hostile, violent, or aggressive behaviour."[68] In 1979, Dr Schauss persuaded two navy officers (Baker and Miller) to test the effects of it on naval cadets and because they agreed, the colour was named after them. This colour was later applied to prison cells as part of a study on its impact.[68] The implementation of Baker-Miller Pink was thought to reduce erratic or hostile behaviour among inmates during the initial phase of confinement.[69] It was also used in various other settings, owing to its perceived calming influence, including psychiatric wards and youth clinics. However, subsequent research revealed that this effect is temporary, lasting only 15-30 minutes.[70] Norwich FC harnessed colour psychology by painting the opposition's changing rooms in this colour intending to lessen their drive... to pacify and soothe them - they were subsequently promoted.[71] The studies done on Baker-Miller pink are now suggested to have a few flaws, but this applied colour psychology shows the understanding and respect we have for colour and the power it holds.

Interestingly, while Baker-Miller Pink initially demonstrated its potential to pacify individuals, later studies unveiled a potential downside - an over-aggressive response from inmates exposed to prolonged periods of this colour. As Karen Haller explains, using the wrong colour, in this case, the wrong pink, along with the proportion used, context and time factors and in balance with other colours, it's likely to elicit unfavourable outcomes.[15]

Yet these dramatic effects can only be created by using a high-quality, full-spectrum light source with a broad variety of wavelengths on-hand to bounce off objects and into our eyes. Colourful light means a colourful space.

Figure 40 | Baker-Miller pink: capable of weakening individuals by up to 35%. If used too much in a space however, it can tip viewers into behaving aggressively.

"A particular pink wavelength can physically weaken individuals by up to 35%![71]"

ORANGE

Exposure to orange light improves alertness and cognitive brain function. Orange stimulates the creative thought process;[73]

YELLOW

Exposure to yellow light can spark muscle energy and mental activity as it catches attention. It is associated with the stomach, liver and intestines, and has been used to treat digestive problems and depression;[15]

There is mounting evidence that light therapy alters the brain in the same way that a drug does.[56] The wavelengths of visible light impact human physiology in different ways, and an absence of any part of the spectrum – through the use of poor lighting – will inhibit a viewer's experience of a space.

For instance, research has shown some of the following effects of exposure to coloured light:

RED

Anti-ageing; its presence increases collagen production to create smoother, younger-looking skin;[72]

"Night-shift work (in which workers are exposed to high doses of blue lights generated by LED lighting) is now classified as "probably carcinogenic" by the World Health Organisation (WHO).[54]"

"It has been reported that adults spend on average just one hour a day outside, which is less than the United Nations' legal requirement for prisoners![50]"

INDIGO

Exposure to this part of the spectrum helps to purify the body, including the blood. It can be used to relieve eye inflammations, ear problems, swelling and extreme pain.[78] Indigo light therapy is reported to help broaden the mind and free it from fears and inhibitions; it can affect us psychologically and have a powerful effect on mental complaints.[79] Its absorption promotes muscle tone, depresses respiration and boosts insensitivity to pain;[80]

VIOLET

Exposure to this colour of light has been found to stimulate the spleen and the building of white blood cells, regulate the tension of blood vessels, and lower blood pressure. It also helps to maintain the potassium-sodium balance in the body.[81] Absorption of violet light has been reported to depress the motor nerves and the lymphatic and cardiac systems, to purify the blood and even to stop tumour growth.[79]

GREEN

:xposure to green light ıelps to create an even skin :omplexion to produce ıaturally beautiful skin.[15] Green-light therapy is eported to reduce pain nd improve the quality of fibromyalgia sufferers' ves, stimulate the creation of growth hormones, trengthen muscles, bones ınd other tissues.[74] It can ncrease the production of encephalins, pain-killing opioid-like chemicals;[75]

BLUE

Treatment with blue light helps to eliminate acne-causing bacteria and whitens teeth.[76] Blue is the counterpart of red. It can be used to lower blood pressure or to calm people;[77]

Creating natural light, artificially

So, what is good light? How do we lift the energy in a room to align the lighting conditions with our biology and give us the best experience? Well, natural light can be considered in terms of five facets, and replication of these can create a biophilically lit environment.

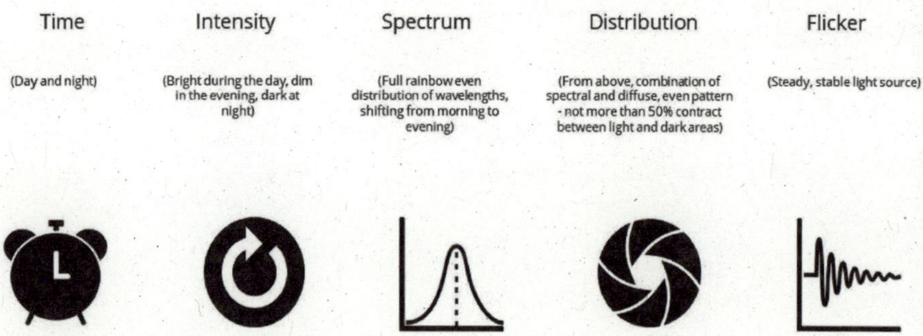

Time

As stated previously, the time we are exposed to light is critical for setting our night/day clock. It is important to ensure that we experience a bright burst of blue light in the morning and avoid it after sunset.

Artificial light sources can now replicate the rising and setting of the sun. Dim-to-warm and tuneable white light sources enable us to adjust the colour of a light source in line with the time of day. The use of such systems in the built environment can dramatically affect the wellness of individuals.

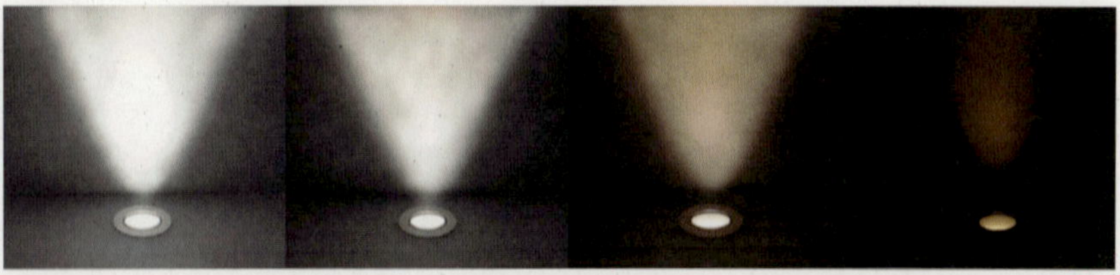

Figure 41 | Tuneable and dim-to-warm lighting.

Intensity

Luminous flux is a measurement used by lighting designers to quantify the total amount of light emitted by a light source, spread over the entire span of the light. We quantify luminous flux in lumens (lm), a photometric unit. The light that shines onto a surface is called illuminance and is measured in lumens per square metre (lm/m^2), which thus measures the brightness of a space. It is also called lux.[82]

Vertical lux vs. horizontal lux

Previously, design industry standards only accounted for horizontal lux, which measured light on flat surfaces such as floors and desks. However, recent approaches consider vertical lux, since most of what we see is in the vertical plane. Light bouncing off walls can directly impact our melanopic response and affect circadian rhythms positively or negatively.[82]

I mentioned previously that natural light is around 50-100 times brighter in the morning than the lighting environment of offices, and typically around 5,000-10,000 times brighter by noon.[50] This has significant effects on the natural systems of employees within a space. On a positive note, we can adapt lux levels to align them with those of the outside world. The WELL building standard, devised by the International WELL Building Institute, quantifies healthy light in equivalent melanopic lux (EML).

It is calculated using the following formula:

EML = vertical lux x light spectral power distribution of a light source

According to the standard, the minimum daytime target should be 200 EML. Without becoming overly concerned with detailed mathematics, the important point is that well-lit spaces require good light on the vertical planes - there is little point in having a brilliantly lit floor with walls that look depressingly dark. It must also be said that legislation is largely outdated and designers are bound to it for legal reasons, not natural ones. If we are to truly craft spaces that support our biology, we must rewrite the legal red tape / guidelines that bind us to a permanence of mundane and unemotional spaces.

Spectrum

As we have seen previously, the absence of any one of the seven colours that make up natural sunlight can have a dramatic effect on our haptic experience of the space we occupy.

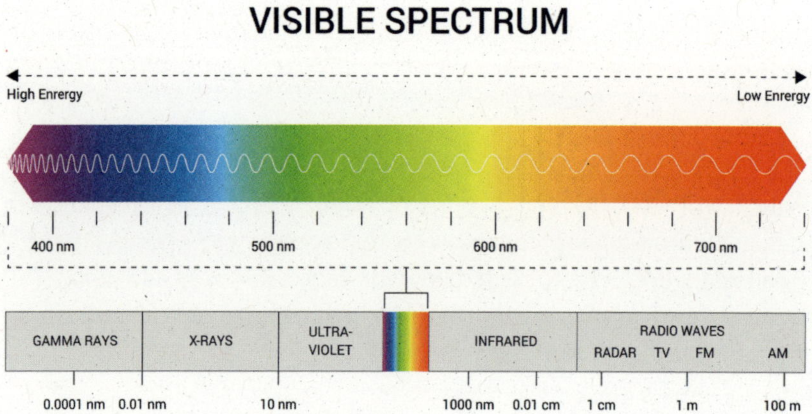

Figure 42 | The visible light spectrum – energetic waves that guide us. Just beyond red is infrared, which we experience as heat. Beyond violet, ultra-violet, which kills MRSA and more.

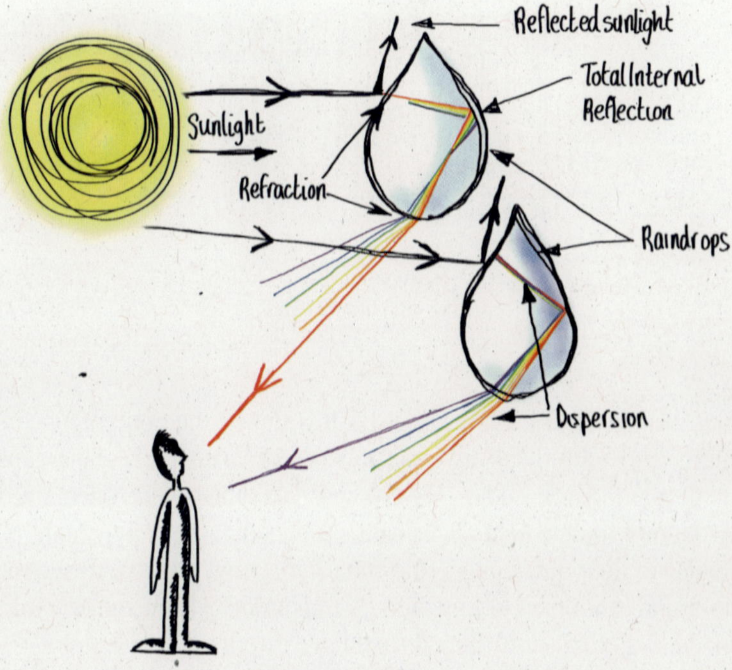

Figure 43 | Sunlight scattering into its individual wavelengths as a result of varying frequencies.

The CRI (colour rendering index) was created in the 1960s by the lighting industry to assess the quality of an artificial light source.[83] The index was intended to assess how natural colours are rendered under an artificial white light source compared with under sunlight. The index has a scale from zero to 100, with a perfect 100 indicating that colours appear the same under the light source as they would in natural sunlight. However, it was based on only 14 colours, so was of limited use in identifying the true quality of an artificial light source.

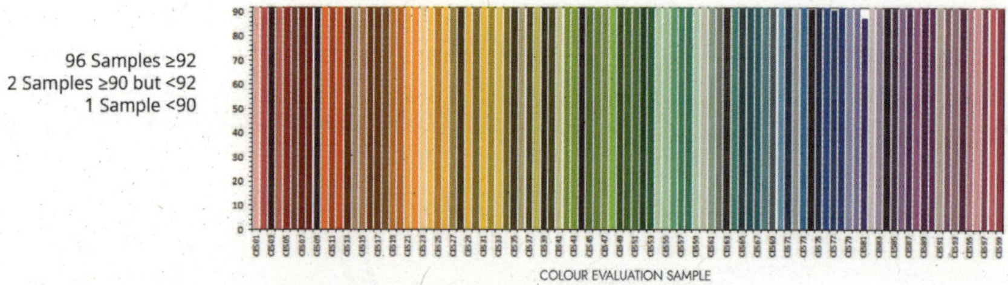

Figure 44 | TM-30-15 values – a better rendering assessment tool with its significantly increased colour testing range.

A new value, TM-30-15, was devised. It widened the comparative colour samples and offered a more comprehensive evaluation of the overall rendition as it was based on 99 colours. Use of this value offers the opportunity to choose artificial light sources that are truly vibrant and biophilic in their distribution. This means it is now possible to see the true colour and emotional connection that an artificial light source can create in a space and bring all the benefits we have discussed to this point. Colours with a high TM-30-15 rating will lift the colours in a space like that of natural light meaning your new house/office refurbishment will sparkle and glimmer just as nature intended.

Figure 45 | The difference light makes in a space. Poor quality LED chip vs a high TM-30-15 LED chip.

Distribution

The eye adjusts like a camera to different light levels, using shadows and contrast to identify forms in space and intuitively prefers spaces with a range of light levels.[84] A bright blast of light can dazzle and confuse the viewer. Contrasting zones of light and darkness, particularly a transitional space such as a corridor, can create an extremely uncomfortable feeling. The lens of the eye adjusts to the brighter areas; as a result, the brain receives insufficient information to make out the darker areas, creating a sense of threatening discomfort and generating a stream of neurotransmitter responses. The eyes move rapidly, the blink reflex is activated and the pupil dilates and contracts.

High-contrast zones affect our ability to move confidently between dark and light areas because the pupil expands and contracts to let in the correct amount of light. It takes up to 30 minutes to fully accommodate differences between bright and dark conditions. When we move from a bright to a dark area, it is hard to see for a moment or two, and we may feel disoriented or caught off-balance. The same is true in reverse, for example, when we have been sitting indoors and then step outside into bright sunshine. This pupil expansion and contraction response becomes slower with age and neurological conditions.[85] The slow speed of the response explains why most trips and falls happen at thresholds or in areas where there is a sharp transition between light and dark areas.[86]

Not only do we prefer scenes that reflect a "natural" luminance distribution from a psychological perspective,[87] there are also practical, physical reasons why scenes that offer soft graduations are easier on the eye and brain.

Figure 46 | Lots of light and shade causes our eyes difficulty as they try to accommodate areas of light and dark.

Because the eye works like a camera - opening and closing to let in the correct amount of light depending on the scene - any super-high-contrast, high-frequency (closely-spaced regular/geometric) patterns that occur in urban or artificial environments pose a problem. The eye cannot work out whether to adapt to the bright or the dark areas.

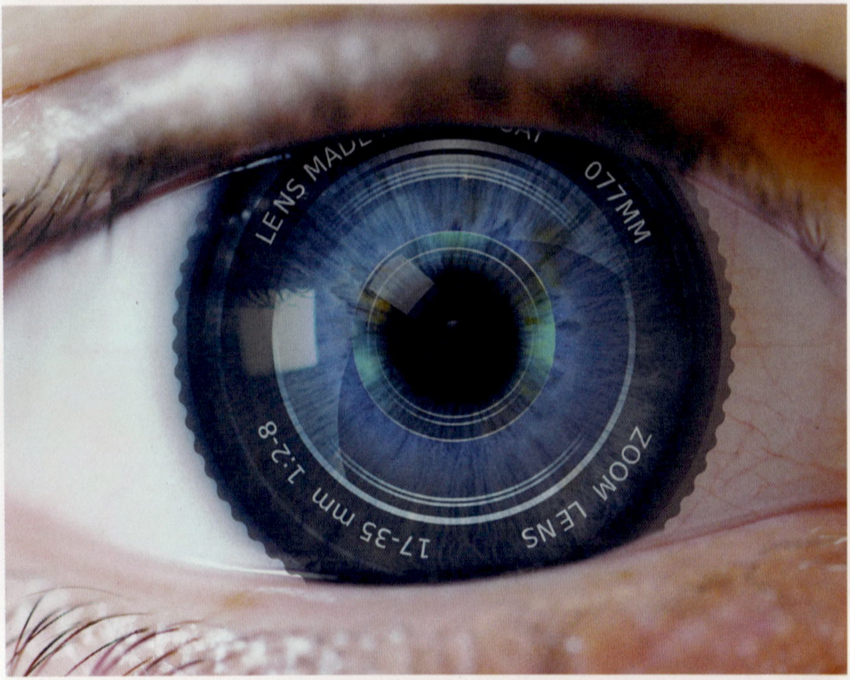

Figure 47 | The eye behaves much like a camera, adjusting its aperture to control the amount of light entering it.

High-contrast lighting also challenges our need for a combination of "prospect and refuge" in an environment: the balance between being able to see around and beyond the space and feeling safe and protected.[88]

Figure 48 | High contrast light and dark creates difficulty for the eye.

The way that light is distributed the light source is extremely important. Too much light without proper control can lead to glare. The built environment contains two types of glare: direct (in which the light shines directly into the eyes) and reflected (in which it bounces off shiny surfaces and screens). The lighting industry has created a "glare rating", which offers a way to measure the level of discomfort that an "average" person would experience in that setting. Different settings have different recommended unified glare ratings (UGRs), but 19 is the threshold in most situations.

Figure 49 | Glare ratings (measured in UGR) and their indicative levels of comfort.

When choosing a light fixture, or luminaire, we can ensure that it is designed to minimise the glare, but there is no substitute for being in the space to experience the light first-hand from different positions and at different times of the day. Choose a luminaire that you can pay full attention to or adjust to fine-tune the effect. Check the position of screens and other reflective surfaces too; light is never experienced in isolation.

Figure 50 | 357 Collin Street – Melbourne. Partner: Light Cubed. Client: Frasers Property. Lighting Designer: ADP Consulting. Architect / Interior Designer: Hames Sharley

"Asking a teenager to get up at 7 am is the equivalent of asking a 50-year-old to get up at 5 am[42]"

Figure 51 | The Stables, Clerkenwell. Soft, diffused light with vibrant colour rendering. A smooth, natural-looking viewing experience. Lighting designer: Gus Goidanich. Photography: Gavriil Papadiotis.

Flicker

The modern LED cannot be dimmed. In order to reduce the overall amount of light emitted, LEDs are turned on and off extremely quickly, which results in a reduction in the average voltage across the LED and, thus, reduced light output. What this means, in essence, is that the LED flickers. Our brains are susceptible to the flickers because they evolved to react to movement up to 1,000 times quicker than our "conscious" mind could, in case a tiny movement represented a predator or threat.[89] So why do we not notice the flickers all the time?

Figure 52 | Flicker in LEDs can cause headaches, fatigue and extreme cases nausea and epilepsy.

As we discussed earlier, a part of the brain known as the superior colliculus is responsible for moving the eyes in short jumps called saccades. Saccades allow the brain to perceive smooth scans of a scene because they stitch together a series of relatively still images.[89] This highly efficient tool also works very hard to remove flicker from a light source. However, it requires significant energy, so it is no surprise that the flicker from LED lights causes headaches, eye strain and even epilepsy.[90] It also reduces reading speed and accuracy.[56] Flicker can be created at any stage in the lighting system, from the power input to the switch (especially dimmer switches) and the luminaire itself.

Steady vision can rarely detect flicker above 90Hz, whereas flicker can be perceived during visual saccades up to or beyond 1kHz.[91] In order to avoid flicker, consult a lighting manufacturer or designer who can guide you through the specification process of control systems, dimming types and wiring. DALI and DMX control are optimal but alternative methods can be implemented effectively with correct guidance from experts on the hardware involved in each circuit. You can also detect flicker in spaces by videoing it using your smartphone under the "slo-mo" setting. If there's flicker in your room, there will be flicker visible on your phone's screen.

Animals and light pollution

A significant element to consider in biophilic lighting is the effect of human activity on the natural world. It is estimated that 80% of Americans can no longer see the Milky Way. Indeed, in 1994, during a blackout, some Los Angeles residents called 911 when they saw the Milky Way for the first time.[92] Light pollution has a huge effect on our environment and is disconnecting us from the wonders of the natural world. LEDs, which are based on blue LEDs, are some of the worst lighting instruments for the environment.

The so-called "blueing effect" enables a blue wavelength to punch through pollution in cities (owing to its high energetic frequency) and to be scattered by it, creating a "sky glow" or halo of light around the city.[93] This adversely affects insects, birds and bats and is the cause of a significant biodiversity emergency.[93]

Figure 53 | Pollution over Canary Wharf, London. LEDs emit significant amounts of blue light, which efficiently bounces through smog, creating domes of light pollution throughout the city.

Other kinds of light pollution also exist: glare, clutter and light trespass. These are less well-known than sky glow but are just as concerning and, arguably, have a greater impact on our daily lives. As we briefly touched upon earlier, glare is excessive brightness that can cause visual discomfort. It is particularly dangerous when driving. Clutter is intense, bewildering and excessive groupings of light sources (for example, Times Square in New York City or London's West End). Light trespass occurs when light seeps into an area where it is unwanted, for example, a street light that illuminates your bedroom or the light from a 24-hour supermarket that spills into your garden.

In areas that experience the greatest light pollution (megacities such as London, for example), we never experience true night. The light level we experience is much closer to twilight than to true dark, which is why starlight is not visible.

In extreme cases, living under round-the-clock artificial light prevents our eyes from adapting fully to the dark. This evolutionary feature enables us to

Figure 54 | A beautiful, clear night sky with no light pollution.

orient ourselves and see vague shapes at night (you may rely on this power when camping, for example).

Sky glow is not sufficiently intense to suppress melatonin production, but it is caused only by the scattering of light from local sources. The direct application of these local sources to humans is much more intense and is probably sufficient to disrupt circadian rhythms. As mentioned previously, the lights inside your home after sunset, particularly if you use bright, white lights, may impact your sleep. Problems with circadian rhythms can lead to illnesses such as obesity, depression and cancer.

What can we do?

Shield street lights

One easy solution is to use fully shielded street lights that are designed to cast light downwards, directing it to where it is needed while minimising glare and sky glow.

Keep light inside

If buildings do not need to be lit up at night, they should not be. The greatest sources of light at night are large commercial buildings that stay open and are populated throughout the night. The designers of these buildings should consider how this light can be directed downwards and prevented from spilling into the sky. In our homes, we can use window coverings such as curtains to prevent the indoor light from escaping to the street, or that from street lights from falling into our bedrooms.

Be inspired by the sunset

We should use light sources that are appropriate to the time of day to protect our circadian rhythms: bright light with high blue content in the morning, and dim, warmer light with low blue content as dusk begins to settle.

Use directional lighting

Designers should avoid up-lighting (particularly outside) and use directional light fittings to light only those things that should be lit. We should ensure that all lighting colours and brightness can be adjusted throughout the day and that lights can be switched off easily and conveniently.

Protect our dark skies

We must protect intrinsically dark landscapes to enable star-gazing and shield wild animals which can become disoriented by artificial light. National parks and nature reserves are rare areas that are largely free of artificial light; these support habitats for native nocturnal creatures.

Sustainable light fixtures: part of a biophilic structure/ ecosystem

Biophilic design is concerned with connecting people to nature in a way that encourages and enhances relationships and responsibilities towards human and natural communities. We live in a world that is both more disconnected and more connected than ever: Deliveroo, Amazon and Uber offer instant gratification yet only minimal connection to people or communities.

Sustainability is a crucial aspect of biophilic design. Creating green spaces, adding water features or plants, and using natural materials can bring a range of benefits. Moreover, products and companies that offer repair services, manufacture locally and offset their own CO_2 can have a significant effect on aligning our space with that of the natural world.

Lighting designers can:

• Know their lighting supplier. We are hard-wired to work with people rather than through a computer. Engaging directly with the supply company will result in better projects, more interesting work and a more specialised specification.

• Go sustainable. Companies can be tested on their sustainability. Choose a certified-B corporation or similarly rated company that has recognised its duty to conserve and perform sustainably.

• Choose natural. Not all products are created equal. Go for natural shapes, finishes, lit effects and customisability to create the most visibly biophilic and vibrant spaces.

Certified B®

reewild

People are naturally tribal. They pursue mutually reinforcing and complementary relationships. Biophilia and biophilic design are concerned with our values and our ethical responsibility to care for and sustain the natural world. Understanding products and connecting to those that look familiar and natural will enrich your relationship with them. This results in material benefits and a host of emotional, intellectual and even spiritual rewards. Sustainable design is biophilic design. Community, sustainability, intellectual development and affection are different parts of this. People can benefit from connections to spaces and objects that have been formed with substance, genuine craft and care. We all understand at an emotional level that knowing the stories about items in a room, such as their design and procurement, significantly impacts the emotional connection we have to that space and the items within it. There is a benefit in creating tribal ecosystems that are local, community-driven and manufactured sustainably.[94]

Figure 55 | Natural shapes and finishes (rust, concrete, limestone and sandstone.)

A statement on light:
The 16th principle of biophilic design?

By now it should be clear just how important light is to our understanding of the world we inhabit. With natural light, we fully experience the world as it is meant to be experienced but, sadly, a fast and potentially world-changing movement is gathering pace. New legislation is forcing many brilliant manufacturers into a corner. This legislation ignores fundamental aspects of the human visual experience and is forcing us to create luminaires with less optical control, higher outputs and a 'mass manufactured' feel. Put simply, we are moving to a world in which spaces will become glaring, flat, devoid of colour and the opposite of what it is to feel biophilic. It is vital that we understand and champion the very best lighting products - and the principles on which they are based - and introduce them to environments with the design expertise of the lighting design community.

On this note, I propose an additional point for the Terrapin principles, or perhaps request that the 6th point ("Dynamic and Diffuse Light") be expanded to include some of the information mentioned in this book to this point.

Building on the already vital point of "dynamic and diffuse lighting" in the existing framework, this 16th principle would highlight the need to control glare, ensure the vibrancy of colours (with high TM-30-15 ratings) and require the ability to adjust and adapt fittings after installation for easy repurposing, recycling and repair. Not only would this make spaces more sustainable in the future, but we would enjoy them more as a result. The ability to tune light to remove blue light in the evenings and add it in the morning is crucial in this respect.

Simplifying this, I propose the inclusion of the five principles of natural light:

Time | Intensity | Spectrum | Distribution | Flicker

with the addition of "adaptable" to make a sixth point relating to future-proofing and repairs on products.

Figure 56 | The use of modular products simplifies the process of optimising lighting within a space, resulting in smoother and more natural illumination. Additionally, maintaining and replacing parts becomes more convenient.

"In 1994, during a blackout, Los Angeles residents called 911 when they saw the Milky Way for the first time.[92]"

SECTION 3

How To:
Terrapin's biophilic design principles

How To: Terrapin's biophilic design principles

This section is adapted from Browning and Ryan's book, *Nature Inside: A Biophilic Design Guide (2020).*[1]

Site context

Designers should consider the ecology of the space: the site's spatial conditions, environmental biodiversity, environment (wind conditions, etc.), plant species, existing architectural conditions, the local community, cultures and colour palette.

Experiential context

What is the building's purpose? Is it a school, residence, office, healthcare centre, or manufacturing or warehouse barn? A knowledge of what happens in the space (for example, refuge spaces, functional spaces, healing spaces, and learning spaces) will help to target experiential goals for the project.

Value proposition

Return on investment. How can employee satisfaction, health improvements, social cohesion, pricing and purchasing behaviour, increased brand identity or market differentiation improve realised benefits?

Biophilic arts and craftsmanship

The use of biophilic arts and craftsmanship offers an opportunity to enhance the sensory experience. The use of quality light, textures, density and visual complexity enables the space to evolve from a visual to a haptic experience (meaning that the person in it can "grasp something" that seems authentic and connecting).

Gap analysis, work-shopping and the narrative

Identify the ultimate outcomes for the inhabitants of a space and realise the gaps to be filled to ensure optimal design. If a space is commercial, how can you create a place in which employees are restored and rested in a way that improves morale, creativity and enthusiasm/performance in the working "zones"? Where are the weak or stress spots? How can these gaps be removed to improve the space?

Figure 57 | Dar Zefta, Lebanon. Lighting Designer: Alta Light. Architect: Simone Kosremelli

Involve the inhabitants to ensure that they are part of the society you are building. Peer reviews help to keep the project aligned. Work out the "why" behind the building's existence. Knowing why you are in a space helps to align the project with its vision and principles.

A breakdown of Terrapin's 15 patterns of biophilic design

Designers have a responsibility - and, more excitingly, an opportunity - to improve the welfare of the inhabitants of the spaces they create. Terrapin's 15 patterns of biophilic design (which inspired the famously worker-focused wellbeing offices at Google) show how this can be done. Each of these points has been proven to improve an individuals performance (by incresaing ability, motivation and opportunity).

Explanations of each follow.

Nature in the space

1. Find a visual connection with nature

Make sure there is a view of an element of nature, living systems or natural processes.

2. Have a non-visual connection with nature

Engage sound, smell, touch or taste.

3. Consider non-rhythmic sensory stimuli

An event or moment that cannot be predicted offers an opportunity for mental rest; for example, birds chirping or branches swinging in the breeze.

4. Thermal and airflow variability.

Create changes in air temperature, relative humidity, airflow across the skin, and surface temperatures that mimic natural environments.

5. Have water present
Enable users of the space to see, hear or touch the water.

6. Dynamic and diffuse light
Vary the intensities and colours of light and use shadow changes over time to mimic conditions that occur in nature.

7. Connect with natural systems
Such links are aimed at triggering a deeper awareness of a functioning ecosystem.

Natural Analogues

8. Biomorphic forms and patterns
Use contours, patterns, textures or numerical arrangements that are found in nature.

9. Material connection to nature
Apply minimal processing to materials and elements from nature so they reflect the local ecology or geology and create a distinct sense of place.

10. Complexity and order
Provide rich sensory information that adheres to a spatial hierarchy that is similar to those encountered in nature.

Nature of the space

11. Prospect
Try to offer an unimpeded view over a distance for surveillance and planning.

12. Refuge
Keep a small portion of a large space for rest, protection or healing.

13. Mystery
Users of the space will be compelled to investigate if there is a mysterious element which provides a sense of anticipation or of being teased.

14. Risk/peril
A feature that appears to offer risk might be dangerous but should be intriguing - even irresistible - and be worth exploring.

15. Awe
Incorporate stimuli that defy an existing frame of reference and lead to a change in perception.

Figure 58 | Iron Fairies, Indonesia. Lighting Designer: Studio Nimmersatt. MNE Consultants: CLA, Indonesia

Part 1 – Nature in the space

1. **Find a visual connection with nature**. A space with a good visual connection to nature feels whole; it grabs our attention and can stimulate or calm those in it. It can convey a sense of time, weather and/or living things. The objective of this pattern is to create an environment that helps the individual shift their focus, relax their eye muscles and temper their cognitive fatigue.

2. **Have a non-visual connection with nature**. A non-visual connection with nature can be provided by thinking of each of your senses:

Sound

Naturally occurring
- Plants/trees
- Façade greening
- Bodies of water
- Animals/insects/fish

Simulated nature

Direct
- Water feature
- Plant wall

Indirect
- Artwork or video depicting a natural scene
- Natural sounds via artificial methods

Scent

Naturally occurring
- Fragrant plants and trees
- Soil/earth

Simulated nature
- Natural plant oils

Touch

Naturally occurring
- Accessible plants/trees
- Accessible water
- Accessible soil/earth

Simulated nature
- Connection to animals
- Natural materials

Taste

Naturally occurring
- Edible plants
- Smells/scents that elicit a taste response

Simulated nature
- Manufactured smells and scents
that create a taste response

3. **Consider non-rhythmic sensory stimuli**. Several factors contribute to establishing accessible and effective non-rhythmic stimuli. As a general guideline, non-rhythmic sensory experiences should occur approximately every 20 minutes for about 20 seconds and, in the case of visual stimuli, from a distance of more than six metres. Such stimuli can be seen in many forms of natural motion, such as reflections in water or the sway of grasses – ever-changing but ever the same.

Many natural stimuli are seasonal, so a strategy that is effective throughout the year, with multiple interventions that overlap with the seasons, will help to ensure that non-rhythmic sensory experiences can occur at any time of the year. In some cases, the intervention may be similar to that of the visual or non-visual connections with nature; what is important is the ephemeral and stochastic quality of the intervention. An intervention that involves the simulation of natural stimuli will probably require collaboration with the mechanical engineer or facilities team early in the design process.

A strategy that involves the use of non-rhythmic stimuli can be interwoven with almost any landscape or horticultural plan. For instance, selecting plant species for window boxes that will attract bees, butterflies and other pollinators may be a more practical application for some projects than maintaining a honey-bee apiary or butterfly sanctuary.

Humans perceive movement in their peripheral view much earlier than they see it straight ahead. The brain then processes the movement of living things in a different place from where it processes the movement of mechanical objects,[2] and this difference leads to the perception that natural movement is generally positive and mechanical movement is neutral or even negative. As a result, the repeated rhythmic motion of a pendulum holds our attention only briefly, the constant repetitive ticking of a clock may come to be ignored over time, and an ever-present scent may lose its mystique with long-term exposure, whereas the stochastic movement of a butterfly will capture our attention each time it occurs, with recurring physiological benefits.

4. **Thermal and airflow variability**. A space with good thermal and air flow variability feels refreshing, active, alive, invigorating and comfortable, offering a sense of both flexibility and control. The intention is that the users can either control their thermal and air flow conditions through individual controls or access variable ambient conditions within a space.

Figure 59 | Mayfair Park Residences. Developers: Clivedale. Lighting Designer: Isometrix. Photography: Gavriil Papadiotis.

The incorporation of air flow and thermal conditions into materials, daylighting, mechanical ventilation and/or fenestration will help the designer to distribute variability over space and time. Thermal comfort is a vital bridging component between biophilic and sustainable design, especially in current conditions of climate change and rising energy costs.

Figure 60 | The Newt, Somerset. Lighting Design: Illumination Works. Photography: Gavriil Papadiotis.

The offer of variable heating and air flow can broaden people's perceptions of thermal comfort and energy demand may be reduced. It has been found that features that allow users to adapt and modify the thermal conditions of their environment increases the range of acceptable temperatures by 2°C above and below the conventional parameters for thermal comfort.[3] However, such a design will require coordination of the design strategies in the project team (e.g., architect, lighting designer and mechanical, electrical and plumbing engineers) at the start of the schematic design process to achieve the designer's intentions.

5. **Include the presence of water**. A space in which water is present feels compelling and captivating. Fluidity, sound, lighting, and the proximity and accessibility of water each contribute to the stimulating or calming effect of a space.

Our interest in water does not diminish with repeated experience, so one small water feature may be adequate. By taking advantage of the sounds created by small-scale running water and our capacity to touch it, we can amplify the desired health response with a multi-sensory experience. Views over large bodies of water, or physical access to natural or designed water bodies, can also have a positive health response as long as they are perceived as unpolluted. Images of nature that include aquatic elements are more likely to help reduce blood pressure and heart rate than similar imagery without water elements.

The designer should prioritise a multi-sensory water experience to achieve the most beneficial outcome. Naturally, fluctuating water movement is better than predictable movement or stagnancy.

High-volume, high-turbulence water features can create discomfort, increase humidity levels or be too noisy, so the proximity of the feature to the people in the space should be considered. Water features can be water- and energy-intensive and should be used sparingly, particularly in climates with little access to water. Shading the water, using high albedo surfaces, and minimising the area of the exposed water surface will reduce water loss through evaporation and could contribute to the biophilic experience.

6. **Dynamic and diffuse light.** Lighting design has long been used to create mood, and the use of different lighting conditions can elicit different psychological responses. The objective of a dynamic and diffuse lighting pattern is twofold: to provide users with lighting options that stimulate the eye and hold attention in a manner that engenders a positive psychological or physiological response, and to help maintain circadian rhythms. The goal should not be to create uniform light distribution throughout an uninteresting space, nor should there be extreme differences that could cause glare or discomfort.

Glare may occur when the lighting difference between adjoining sources or surfaces has a brightness or luminance ratio of greater than 40:1, which diminishes visual comfort.[5] For work areas, luminance ratios between the area where the task is being performed and the immediate surroundings should not exceed 10:1. So, while dramatic lighting differences may work well in certain religious, socialising or circulation spaces, they are not ideal for work surfaces. Diffuse lighting on vertical and ceiling surfaces provides a calm backdrop to the visual scene. Accent lighting together with another layering of light sources creates interest and depth, while task or personalised lighting provides localised flexibility in intensity and direction. These layers help to create a pleasing visual environment.[5]

The movement of light and shadows along a surface can attract our attention, such as the dappled light under the canopy of an oak tree or the reflections of rippling water on a wall. These patterns tend to be fractals, and the brain is attuned to moving fractals. Just as variations in lit surfaces help us interpret them, conduct various tasks and navigate safely, circadian lighting is important in supporting biological health. The quality of the user experience is improved by leveraging opportunities for illuminance fluctuation, light distribution and colour variability that stimulate the human eye without causing discomfort.

Design considerations to establish a balance between dynamic and diffuse lighting conditions include the following:

• Dynamic lighting conditions can help create a smooth transition between indoor and outdoor spaces.

• Extreme dynamic lighting conditions - such as sustained movement, changing colours, direct sunlight penetration and high contrasts - may not be appropriate for spaces in which directed attention activities are performed.

• Circadian lighting is especially important in spaces that people occupy for extended periods.

Figure 61 | SOMA, located on Denman St, Soho. Photography: Gavriil Papadiotis. Architectural Designers: Cake Architecture

7. **Connect with natural systems**. The connection with natural systems is aimed to heighten both an awareness of natural properties and our environmental stewardship of the ecosystems within which these properties prevail. The strategy for working with such patterns may be as simple as identifying key content in a view of nature (e.g. deciduous trees in the garden or blossoming orchids on the window sill), or it may be a more complex integration of systems, such as highlighting the relationship between building occupant behaviour and rainwater infrastructure capacity (e.g. rain gardens, bioswales, storm sewers) by regulating domestic activities (e.g. showering, laundry) during rain events. In either case, the temporal component is usually the key factor in pattern recognition that triggers a heightened awareness of a functioning ecosystem.

Design considerations and opportunities that may help to create quality connections with natural systems include:

• A landscape design that responds to rain events;

• The provision of visual access to existing natural systems - the easiest and most cost-effective approach;

• The incorporation of responsive design into the integration of rainwater capture and treatment (e.g. use of materials that change form or expand function with exposure to solar heat gain, wind, rain/moisture or shading);

• Structures (e.g. steps, wells); and

• Land formations (e.g. bioswales, arroyos, dunes).

Interactive design should also be considered, especially for children, patients or the elderly (such as an integrative educational curriculum, horticulture programmes, community gardens, seasonal cooking/diet).

Figure 62 | The Spine, Royal College of Physicians, Liverpool. Architect: AHR. Lighting Designer: Mary Rushton-Beales. Photography: Paul Karalius.

Figure 63 | Tower of London, Bloom. Client: Historic Royal Palaces. Landscape Design: Grant Associates Lighting Design: 18fifty and Nipek

Part 2 – Natural analogues

8. **Biomorphic forms and patterns**. Biomorphic forms and patterns have evolved from research on view preferences,[6] how stress can be reduced through inducing a shift in focus, and how concentration can be enhanced. We have a visual preference for organic and biomorphic forms, although we have not yet formulated why this is the case in scientific terms. While our brain knows that biomorphic forms and patterns are not living things, we may describe them as symbolic representations of life.[7]

There are no right angles or straight lines in nature. The golden angle, approximately 137.5°, is the angle between successive florets in some flowers, while curves and angles of 120° are frequently exhibited in other elements of nature.[8]

The Fibonacci series (0, 1, 1, 2, 3, 5, 8, 13, 21, 34...) is a numeric sequence that occurs in many living things, especially plants. Phyllotaxy, or the spacing of plant leaves, branches and flower petals (so that new growth does not block the sun or rain from older growth), often follows the Fibonacci series. Related to the Fibonacci series is the golden mean (or golden section) - a ratio of 1:1.618 that occurs time and again among living forms that grow and unfold in steps or rotations, such as the arrangement of seeds in sunflowers or the spiral of a seashell.

Biomorphic forms and patterns can be applied either as cosmetic or decorative components of a larger design or integrated into the structural or functional design. The two approaches can be utilised in tandem to enhance the biophilic experience.

Figure 64 | Dolmen Residents
Products: DecoStrip & DecoFlex
Lighting Designer: Light360
Photographer: Sara Pickering

Figure 65 | Hand polished antique bronze bezels

Figure 66 | Phos mood board - satin and polished copper light fittings and mesh from our sister company, Cadisch MDA.

Quality biomorphic design can involve application on two or three planes or dimensions (e.g. the floor and wall planes; furniture windows and soffits) for greater diversity and frequency of exposure. However, overuse of forms and patterns should be avoided as this may lead to visual toxicity. Comprehensive interventions are more cost-effective if they are introduced early in the design process.

9. **Material connection to nature**. A space with a good material connection with nature feels rich, warm, authentic and, sometimes, stimulating. People are intrigued by nature and how it changes, adapts and ages over time. In buildings, this sort of change and ageing can be accomplished through the use of organic materials that are susceptible to weathering and colour change, so that we observe slight changes in our built environment over time.

Natural materials can be decorative or functional, typically processed or extensively altered (e.g. wood planks, granite countertops) from their original "natural" state. While they may be extracted from nature, they are only analogous to the items in their "natural" state. To create a quality material connection, quantities of a (natural) material and colour should be specified based on the space's intended function (e.g. to restore calm or to stimulate).

Figure 67 | Phos Eyeconic Mini Trim Adjustable. Finish: plated antique brass.

Figure 68 | Phos Trimless Nano Eyeconic. Finish: olive green (custom RAL).

Similarly, a degree of variability in materials and applications is recommended rather than high ratios of any material or colour. Real or minimally processed materials are preferred over synthetic variations because human receptors can distinguish between real and synthetic.

Incorporation of the colour green may help to enhance creative environments; however, most scientific studies on the impact of this colour have been conducted in controlled laboratory environments, so any dependence on colour to engender creativity should be considered experimental.

Many natural colours, or earth tones, are subdued tones of brown, green or blue. The colours in buildings should represent these natural tones. Bright colours should be used sparingly - one study found that red flowers on plants were fatiguing and distracting to occupants.[9]

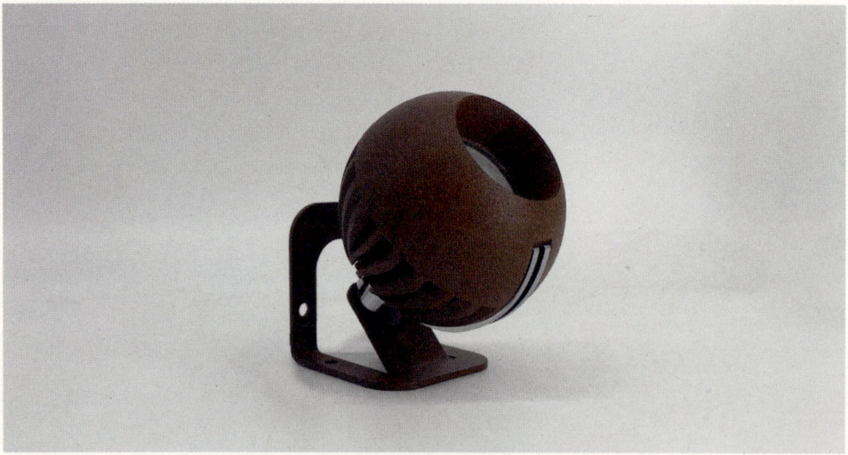

Figure 69 | Orba Interior Internal Corner. Finish: speciality powder coated, rust

10. Complexity and order. Complexity and order offer rich sensory information that adheres to spatial hierarchies similar to those encountered in nature. For instance, interactions of multiple wallpaper patterns, complex patterns in carpets and moiré patterns in seating fabrics have been found to cause these surfaces to seem to move as occupants walk through the space and, therefore, potentially cause extreme visual perception problems.[10] Complexity and order should aim to provide symmetries and fractal geometries that align in a natural spatial hierarchy to create a visually nourishing environment that engenders a positive psychological or cognitive response.[1]

Figure 70 | Omar's Place. Trimless Eyeconic Adjustable downlights in a tuba brass finish. Complexity and order in action.

To create quality complexity and order patterns, the following should be taken into account:

• Prioritise artwork and material selection, architectural expressions, landscape, and master planning schemes that reveal fractal geometries and hierarchies;

• Fractal structures with iterations of three will have more impact than a design limited to two iterations;

• Computer technology that uses the algorithms of mathematical and geometric functions can easily produce fractal designs for architectural, design and planning applications. If a fractal design is being created, consider using geometries with a mid-range dimensional ratio (broadly speaking, 1.3-1.75);

• Plan the use of fractals carefully. Overuse of and/or extended exposure to high-fractal dimensions can instil discomfort or even fear, rather than the intended aim to nourish and reduce stress. However, the avoidance or under-utilisation of fractals in design can result in predictability and a lack of interesting features;

• Those designing a new building or landscape should consider its impact on the fractal quality of the existing urban skyline.

Figure 71 | Casa Cruz, London
Lighting Designer: Stileman Lighting

Part 3 – Nature of the space

11. **Prospect**. The prospect from a window reminds us of our beginnings. According to evolutionary psychology, we should prefer habitats similar to the African savannas on which we evolved. The objective of the prospect pattern is to provide users with a condition suitable for the visual surveying and contemplation of the surrounding environment for both opportunities and hazards.

Figure 72 | Original Bathrooms, Richmond.

There are potentially endless combinations in which the characteristics of prospect can be applied[12] and interior, exterior, short-depth and high-depth prospects can coincide. This complexity and variety make prospects a powerful design element. In interior or dense urban spaces, the prospect is the ability to see from one space to another. It is strengthened when there are clear distinctions and the opportunity to see through multiple spaces.[13]

A quality prospect design could involve:

• The orientation of buildings, fenestration, corridors and workstations to optimise visual access to indoor or outdoor vistas, activity hubs or destinations;

• Design with or around an existing or planned savanna-like ecosystem, body of water and evidence of human activity or habitation. These will help to increase the richness of information in the prospect view;

• The provision of focal lengths of ≥ six metres, preferably 30 metres; when a space has sufficient depth, spatial properties can be leveraged to enhance the experience by removing visual barriers. The limitation of partition heights to about three metres will provide spatial barriers while allowing seated occupants a view across a space. Understorey vegetation or hedges should use a similar guide; preferred height limitations will depend on the terrain and how the space is experienced most frequently (e.g. while sitting, standing or on a bicycle);

• Positioning stairwells at the building perimeter with a glass façade and interior glass stairwell walls can produce a dual prospect;

• In rooms with high ceilings, the elevation of perimeter or interior spaces by 30-40cm enhances the prospect condition;

• The quality of the view and the balance between prospect and refuge are often more important than the size or frequency of the experience;

• Consideration of the visual connection with nature discussed in Point 1 will optimise the prospect experience with a quality view.

12. **Refuge**. A good refuge area feels safe and provides a sense of retreat and withdrawal - for work, protection, rest or healing - whether alone or in small groups. It feels unique and separate from its surrounding environment; its spatial characteristics may feel contemplative, embracing and protective without disengaging its occupants.

Figure 73 | Radisson Blu. Refuge spaces to relax and rejuvenate. Designer: OMO Design

Refuge conditions are important in enabling people to feel refreshed and thereby reduce their stress levels and lower blood pressure and heart rates. Other benefits of refuge areas are reduced irritation, fatigue and perceived vulnerability, as well as improved concentration, attention and perception of safety.[14, 15, 16, 17]

The primary objective of the refuge is to provide users with an easily accessible and protective environment - a smaller portion of a larger space - that supports rest and recharge. The secondary objective is to keep this space barely visible from the outside. The principal spatial condition is protection overhead and to the user's back, preferably on three sides. The strategic placement or orientation of the space can also influence the quality of the experience.

Common functions of refuges are:

• To provide weather or climate protection;

• To offer protection from physical danger;

• To be a place in which to speak privately or to take some time out without being seen;

• A space for reflection, meditation, rest or relaxation;

• A reading area;

• An area for complex thinking.

Figure 74 | Fitzrovia, London. Designer: Studio Hopwood

In most cases, the refuge is not entirely enclosed but provides some contact (visual or aural) with the surrounding environment for surveillance by those inside. The greater the number of protective sides, the greater the sense of refuge; however, complete refuge - protection on all sides - is not necessarily the most appropriate or effective design, as it does not maintain a relationship with the larger space. The traditional lean-to is a good example of a basic refuge, as is a cosy bench seat in a kitchen bay window or a fireside inglenook.

Refuge spaces take many forms, so design decisions require that the designer understands the context and defines the intended user experience. Endless combinations of design elements can create a quality refuge space that offers shade or protection from natural or human-made environmental conditions.

Designers of refuges must consider the following:

• Low ceiling conditions usually characterise indoor refuge spaces. For spaces that have standard ceiling heights other than in the refuge, the low ceiling may be approximately 45-60cm below the main ceiling; often, this height is achieved through the use of treatments such as a soffit, a drop-ceiling or acoustic panelling, or suspended fabric;

• For outdoor or indoor spaces with particularly high ceilings (>five metres), a more drastic differential may be needed to achieve the desired outcome. Examples include freestanding or vegetative alcoves and mezzanine-like structures;

• More than one type of refuge space may be needed to address the various needs of large populations or multiple activity types. Such requirements can be met through the use of different spatial dimensions, lighting conditions and degrees of concealment;

• Light levels in refuge spaces should differ from those of adjacent spaces; user lighting controls can broaden the functionality of the refuge space.

Figure 75 | BXR London is the City's first high-end, boutique boxing gym. Lighting Designer: DHA Designs. Photography: Peter Fordham.

13. **Mystery**. The promise of more information, achieved through partially obscured views or other sensory devices, encourages the individual to travel deeper into the environment. It provides a sense of anticipation, of being teased, and compels users to investigate the space further. The mystery pattern is based on the idea that people have two basic needs in an environment: to understand and to explore.[18] Mystery characterises a place in which an individual feels compelled to move forward to see what is around the corner; it is the partially revealed view ahead. The objective of the mysterious space is to provide a functional environment that encourages exploration and supports stress reduction and cognitive restoration. Other "nature of the space" patterns can be experienced from a stationary position, but mystery implies movement and analysis starting from a place that is perceived positively.

Mystery conditions exist in transitory spaces such as indoor and outdoor plazas, corridors, pathways and parks. The sense of mystery can be diluted over time and with routine exposure; however, strategies that include revolving content or information – such as windows into common areas where activity is constantly changing – are most effective in spaces that are routinely occupied by the same group of people.

Designers of mystery spaces should consider the use of curving edges, which slowly reveal what lies ahead and are more effective than sharp corners in drawing people through a space. Dramatic shade and shadows can enhance the mystery experience, but dark areas or shallow depths of field can instil unwelcome feelings of surprise or fear. The speed at which users transit through a space influences the choice of aperture and area size; a faster transition typically means a larger entrance and space.

Organically evolving mystery conditions (e.g. low-maintenance gardens with winding paths) will change their characteristics over time. These changes should be monitored, as they may enhance or degrade the sense of mystery as it evolves into a surprise area (e.g. overgrown plantings will obscure the depth of field).

14. **Risk/peril**. A space that creates a sense of risk or peril will exhilarate the visitor while carrying an implied threat; it may be even a little mischievous or perverse. The person within it feels that it may be dangerous but finds it intriguing – possibly even irresistible – and, hence, worth exploring. The idea behind the risk/peril pattern is to arouse attention and curiosity and to refresh memory and problem-solving skills. Different degrees of risk can be incorporated into a design depending on the intended users and space available; a cantilevered walkway over a sheer cliff is an extreme case, while viewing a predator in a zoo exhibit may provide a greater sense of control, and rock-hopping through a gentle water feature risks only wet feet.

Figure 76 | Passing under Michael Heizer's "Levitated Mass" at Los Angeles County Museum of Art may make your heart skip a beat, a great example of the "risk and peril" biophilic pattern. Credit: Craig Dietrich. License: cc by 2.0.

A quality risk/peril area requires careful design. These interventions are usually deliberate and the chosen design must be appropriate for the particular user group or place. An element of safety must protect users from harm while still allowing the experience of risk. As with other design features, strategies that rely on spatial conditions are easier to implement when incorporated into the conceptual design and schematic phases of the design process.[15]

15. **Awe**. Stimuli that defy an existing frame of reference and lead to a change in perception. Frank Lloyd Wright mastered this in his spatial designs by using "compression and release" to generate feelings of bewilderment. His designs lead users to move from small compressed spaces into larger, wider ones, generating awe-inspiring spatial releases.

SECTION 4

Case Studies / Inspiration

SPEIRS
MAJOR

SPEIRS MAJOR LIGHT ARCHITECTURE

The Psychology of Light

1.0 Light for Wellbeing, Enjoyment and Experience

Designing with light to enhance people's enjoyment and experience is a central part of our ethos. Beyond simply providing visual acuity where natural light is insufficient, lighting has the power to transform our perception of a space, fundamentally impact the experience of our environment and change our behaviour. When we design with light, we consider much more than making individual elements appear attractive: we aim for our lighting design to be greater than the sum of its parts and to have a meaningful impact.

The dictionary definition of 'wellness' is described as the state of being comfortable, healthy or happy. Lighting considerations for physiological comfort include providing task-appropriate light levels and avoiding glare and flicker, while considering the diverse and changing needs of the population. Lighting for psychological comfort creates a sense of safety and security that may be fostered by easy wayfinding and navigation, good facial recognition and spatial legibility, all of which form the basis of a well-designed lighting solution.

When we think about how light impacts our health, the most significant influence is natural light, which affects our circadian rhythms. It follows that the greatest direct influence we can have on health is working with architects to help ensure that users receive sufficient exposure to natural light.

As lighting designers, we believe that happiness is the aspect of wellbeing that we can most influence. For us this is best described through the visual, emotional and social connections that light reinforces; the way that light makes us feel and behave: the psychology of light.

1.1 Visual connections

Darkness delivers us a blank canvas. In being selective in what we light and how we light it, we can choreograph where the eye is drawn, reinforcing connections or providing visual cues.

Views

Lighting elements of the landscape after dark extends our connection with nature, especially when these are viewed from inside a building, lengthening our visual field and boosting our biophilic connection.

Reflective globes of light embedded within the planting of K11 Discovery Park in Hong Kong help to extend the view out from the café after dark. © SMLA, K11 Discovery Park, Jackie Chan.

Storytelling

We use light to express the narrative of a place or a building, visually connecting people to the ideas and the stories embedded in their design and fabric.

The animated light on the BIO4 renewable power plant in Copenhagen evokes a sense of the energy and natural light filtering through the 'forest' inspired façade. © SMLA, Bio4, AllanToft.

Wayfinding

Lighting helps to make a space more legible. By carefully selecting landscape or building elements to light, we create visual markers that help people to navigate intuitively and confidently.

A blend of light and darkness supports safe, intuitive wayfinding at the Green Heart, University of Birmingham, UK. © SMLA, Green Heart, James Newton.

1.2 Connection with the Surrounding Environment

Mindfulness is the practice of being fully present and engaged in the moment. In all our projects we engage closely with how materials, light and people interact, looking for ways to elevate the experience and gently encouraging people to take notice of the fabric of their environment.

Focus

In choreographing a hierarchy of focus using different intensities and qualities of light, we draw people's attention to selected details and aspects of a design.

Our design for the exterior of the iconic Battersea Power Station in London features close offset warm light to reveal and enhance the heritage brickwork. © SMLA, Battersea Power Station, Peter Landers.

Amplification

Light can be used to boost the presence or effect of elements within the environment to create a more powerful experience.

In Queen Elizabeth II Park in London, we extended the experience of walking through the avenue of trees using dappled light to fill the pathway, immersing visitors in light. © SMLA, Queen Elizabeth Olympic Park, James Newton.

Transformation

Light has the power to completely change our perception of a space. By adjusting the balance of intensities and quality of light across different surfaces and materials, we can create apparent shifts in dimension, volume, and ambience.

The lighting scenes we designed for the monastery in Pannonhalma, Hungary, provide cues for visitors' behaviour, indicating time for quiet contemplation, communal gathering, or wondrous appreciation. © SMLA, Pannonhalma Monastery, James Newton.

Personal Control

Where possible, allowing a degree of local control over the lighting can elicit a greater sense of ownership and sense of ease in a space.

At Maggie's Cancer Care Centre in Newcastle, northern UK, we enabled visitors to control reading lights in the library and the lighting within each room, tuning the atmosphere to suit their needs and mood. © SMLA, Maggies Newcastle, James Newton.

1.3 Emotional connections

In many projects, we intend the positive effects of lighting to be felt at a subconscious level. In some instances, we choose to explicitly to create a moment of delight.

Surprise

Providing an element of magic coming from light in an unexpected place or time can have a powerful and positive effect on our mood.

For the K11 Art and Cultural Centre in Hong Kong, we dynamically programmed light to appear to cascade down the glazed façade, like an eruption of fireworks. © SMLA, K11 Art and Cultural Centre, Jeff Tung.

Contemplation

We design some lighting to support a moment of pause and reflection, offering respite from busy surroundings or the hectic pace of life.

Our temporary light art piece 'Half Life' for the Kings Cross Tunnel in London engaged busy commuters over a period of weeks, encouraging them to engage with and consider the evolving and dissolving light. © SMLA, HalfLife, James Newton.

Playfulness

Occasionally, we create exuberant designs purely with the aim of raising a smile.

UK television Channel 4's Big 4 sign featured umbrellas transformed with light into a joyous kaleidoscope of colour. © SMLA, Channel 4.

1.4 Social connections

Light can act as a subtle or subliminal guide, influencing how we behave in a space. We can use light to encourage different behavioural patterns and encourage greater social interaction.

Place-making

By making people feel more relaxed and safe, light facilitates opportunities for social interaction in cities and within buildings, fostering a sense of belonging and community.

The pools of warm light we created over the benches in Elephant Park, South London, have become popular spots to socialise after dark, while not over lighting the park. © SMLA, Elephant Park, James Newton.

Movement

Our eyes are naturally drawn to brightly lit, colourful, or animated surfaces and this can subtly encourage people to move in a different way.

In the Macquarie Bank HQ, London, the dramatic red light on the red-painted central stairwell led to people using the stairs more, resulting in both social and health benefits. © SMLA, Macquarie Bank.

Character

The colour temperature, intensity and distribution of light all contribute to how people feel and behave.

The warm soft lighting and zones of pooled light in the JW3 Community Centre in North London create a sense of comfortable intimacy ideal for socialising. © SMLA, JW3 Community Centre, James Newton.

1.5 Connection with Nature

We are inspired by nature and often use effects that evoke some level of connection with the natural world.

Dynamism

Bringing a sense of the diurnal and seasonal shifts in intensity and tone found in daylight to our designs helps them to feel fresh and natural.

In the café of 100 Liverpool Street, London, we used tuneable white light above cloudlike ceiling panels, shifting the atmosphere to recall the shifting tones of the sky. © SMLA, 100 Liverpool Street, James Newton.

Colour and Texture

Whether it is fractal forms of leaves and flowers or a view of the horizon, connections with nature are calming and improve concentration. We draw attention to and amplify the colour and texture of the natural elements in a design to contribute to the subconscious benefits that the space can provide.

In Aldermanbury Square, London, the strong lighting accents on the shuttered concrete wall reveal the timber impressions from the original boards. © SMLA, Aldermanbury Square, James Newton.

Darkness

Just as we are tuned to natural light, we need darkness to provide balance and to provide moments of visual relief. We incorporate darkness into our lighting design to allow us to create the greatest impact with the least amount of light, helping to protect biodiversity, minimise our impact on the planet and provide some visual quietude.

1.6 Connection with Nature

On every project we work on, we remind ourselves that the only reason we are designing lighting is for people to benefit from it in some way. By understanding people better, we feel we can design better lighting. The psychology of light is therefore at the core of our design ethos.

In Exchange Square, central London, we kept general light levels as low as possible, channeling focus on low seating areas where people gather to socialise and benefit from the calming influence of the flow of water and light. © SMLA, Exchange Square, James Newton.

dark source

DARK SOURCE

At no point in our history, have we produced and consumed light more than now. This has led light pollution to increase at an alarming rate impacting on our health, nocturnal biodiversity and the environment whilst reshaping our perception of the night. Light pollution is not only environmental, it is also a cultural problem. Even the terms we use for communicating light such as 'brightness' and 'darkness' can be very subjective from both cultural and individual perspectives. Mechanically, it may be easy to switch something off but culturally doing so is challenging. Dark sky also represents quiet skies & landscapes offering a refuge for the well-being of all earthlings suffering from the abundance of electric light at night. Hence the reason, Dark Source sought to develop practical precedents in which the judicious and considerate use of light is applied in the context of working with committed, inventive communities who have striven to restore and protect their dark skies.

Plas y Brenin, Snowdonia, Wales / UK

Plas y Brenin is a centre for outdoor sports located in Snowdonia, North Wales, and designated a Dark Sky Reserve in 2015. It had suffered from a significant level of light pollution that was visible for miles, negatively affecting the environmental and aesthetic qualities of its surroundings. This stirred the National Park Authority, in collaboration with Prosiect Nos - the North Wales Dark Sky Partnership which aims to create a vast area of protected dark skies - to commission Dark Source to develop a lighting design to restore the dark skies. The aim was to install dark sky-friendly lighting to create an inviting ambience and experience without condemning people to move and rest in conditions of pitch-black darkness.

Prosiect Nos has developed a unique approach to tackling light pollution. It raises funds and targets the light polluters in the area, offering them site-specific, dark sky-friendly lighting solutions and facilitating implementation of the proposals. This partnership is an effective and practical method which achieves quick and eye-catching results.

The Plas y Brenin project highlighted an environmental ethos that aimed to reduce energy waste and impacts on biodiversity while exploring further opportunities to enhance the night-time experience. As in many other cases, budgets for dark sky projects are low, encouraging designers to push the boundaries of creativity within the limited financial means available. Initially envisaged as a car park lighting improvement scheme, the project expanded into a more holistic programme that covered the whole site. After investigating the relative costs of a diverse range of luminaires offered by international suppliers, budget decisions were made that ensured the best value for money.

The existing lighting consisted primarily of fluorescent bulkheads and LED floodlights, reducing the site's legibility, and glare and uncontrolled light dispersal across the space shaped the visual experience. Moreover, the lighting was unevenly distributed, with certain areas over-lit and others deprived of light. Accordingly, the holistic approach devised sought to strike a balance between lit and unlit spaces to create a visually pleasant and consistent experience. As part of this goal, warm-coloured, glare-free, low-intensity lighting was utilised to meet dark sky-friendly measures and create a more inviting atmosphere, while the imperative to maximise high energy efficiency ensured that longer-term costs would not be exceeded (Figure 2).

The majority of the recently installed lighting at Plas y Brenin is situated below eye level and at door height. Illumination is located on a human scale by focusing on the diffusion of light across the horizontal plane. As a result, all lighting is accessible for ease of maintenance and is able to meet high standards in exterior rating and durability. In certain areas,

vertical illumination was essential to reinforce the legibility of the site and facilitate effective wayfinding, and, in these cases, it was ensured that luminaires faced downwards to avoid upward travelling light. Moreover, to create a textured visual character unique to the site, luminaires with elliptical and forward throw were used, increasing reach and coverage. Besides the installation of a range of new luminaires, all floodlights were removed from the site. Responsive illumination was also fitted at all the entrance thresholds that are marginal to the flows and circulations of human bodies, and passive infrared sensors (PIR) were introduced to avoid the unnecessary illumination of these non-essential areas, with lights only coming on after dark and when movement is detected. Thus, at times of no activity, light was not wasted.

This use of PIR technology was also extended to areas where supplying mains power proved challenging, with solar lanterns deployed as a low-energy solution. To fulfil objectives to minimise material and economic waste, existing bollard bodywork was refurbished and maintained so that only light sources were replaced.

The imposition of standardised forms of lighting has often discouraged inventive solutions, with restrictions on lumen, height and distribution restricting the capacity of creative, place-specific measures to enhance nocturnal environments. However, at Plas y Brenin, the potential to introduce innovative illumination was facilitated by the fact that the site is privately owned, allowing lighting standards to be partially relaxed. The focus thus moved away from conceiving luminaires as stand-alone items, and functionally replacing outworn and inappropriate fixtures, towards the visualisation of a cumulative effect promoting a holistic perspective that guided how the site would look and feel. This degree of freedom in design also inspired the careful arrangement of multiple layers of light that met dark sky-friendly criteria and created an inviting night-time experience. In terms of the latter, visitors who are already attuned to exploring the darkness through adventure sports activities are lured outside, advancing the goal of achieving greater social sustainability by offering people external spaces to inhabit.

Gratifyingly, the new lighting scheme did not only impact upon the social, aesthetic and environmental qualities relevant to humans; it also encouraged the return of bats to the site to forage in the hedgerows that were formerly too brightly illuminated. By looking at the wider picture, the project has ensured that a core area of the Dark Sky Reserve is further enhanced and protected, offering a night-time experience aligned with Plas y Brenin's brand and environmental ethos.

The overall transition to LEDs has maximised the longevity of the scheme and achieved energy savings through the installation of a wide range of highly efficient lighting products, with energy usage reduced by 1.9 tonnes of CO2e (8,000kW) annually. The multi-award-winning project has also served as an exemplar for other environmentally or dark sky-oriented lighting schemes, particularly following a recent report on BBC One's Countryfile programme that has extended awareness of the important role of considerate lighting design within the dark skies movement.

Figure 1 | Images illustrating the significantly reduced impact of replacement lighting in Plas y Brenin, Snowdonia, Wales.

dark source

DARK SOURCE

Newport, Mayo, Ireland

With large areas only scantly populated, Ireland has huge potential for the assignation of dark sky areas. These possibilities have been adopted at Newport, a town with ambitious aspirations to become the first dark sky community in Ireland. Located within the Wild Nephin National Park, which becomes the Mayo Dark Sky Park after nightfall, the town aims to establish an important precedent in shifting preconceptions and confirming that populated settlements can also become valuable dark sky destinations. In this regard, Newport Dark Sky Masterplan seeks to inspire other communities to follow its example by broadcasting its past achievements and future targets and showcasing the full extent of how much can be accomplished through the deployment of considerate illumination.

By the time Dark Source became involved, the community had already established a clear vision to develop a dark sky master plan with a holistic and dark sky-friendly approach to lighting design. The scheme also sought to create an aesthetically enhanced night-time environment through illumination, thus ensuring social and visual sustainability as well as environmental value. As part of this project, two iconic architectural landmarks, St. Patrick's Church and the Seven Arches Bridge, were identified as sites at which lighting redesign could eliminate the light pollution and visual discomfort currently caused by poor illumination.

The first phase of the project focused on replacing the glaring floodlighting around St. Patrick's Church, which was illuminated by luminaires that diminished the beautiful heritage architecture of the 100-year-old building. Visible from numerous points in the town, its hilltop location exacerbated the adverse effects of the poor lighting, with large quantities of wasted glare ascending into the sky without bringing out the ornamental features of the church's façade. Formerly illuminated by sodium lighting, the floodlighting

has been replaced with LEDs but, as in so many cases, without consideration of the environmental harm of such lighting on non-humans and humans. The project not only sought to change the lights one by one but reconsidered the conception of the lighting in order to future-proof the design and thus avoid perpetuating environmental problems in the future.

The project has also been grasped as an opportunity to change the relationship between the church and its surroundings. Previously, vertical façade lighting had shaped the visual emphasis on how the church was seen at night, and this was inverted by emphasising the horizontal ground plane. We have reinstalled lanterns on the railings of the perimeter which better show the heritage fabric of the church both by day and night. These lanterns are designed to provide a warm colour temperature (2,200K) and subtly illuminate the church periphery without causing glare. This has encouraged the public to visit and explore the church grounds after dark without the dazzling floodlights that inhibited movement.

On the church itself, we explored the potential of emphasising key architectural elements by replacing the formerly undifferentiated illumination of the building's façades. This was accompanied by the decision to make more substantive use of the interior lighting of the church, which the removal of the glaring façade illumination revealed more clearly (Figure 2). In addition, we introduced a switch-off time to allow a period of rest for both the environment and the architecture, and so that the impressive, silhouetted form of the darkened church can stand out against the night sky, adding a different dimension to its visual impact.

Beyond the church, we are currently negotiating street lighting standards, helping the project to save significant money and energy while ensuring that the illumination installed is more respectful of the darkness of the night. The need to persuade key agencies, primarily the local authority and the highways authority, has involved communicating measurements of existing lux levels, which reveal that the current street lighting exceeds requirements.

Figure 2 | Considered lighting for St Patrick's Church makes its different architectural features more distinctive while also providing added emphasis to the ground plane in Newport, Mayo, Ireland.

In light of this finding, we have argued for the deployment of a new dimming strategy which would meet a more realistic safety standard while offering greater energy savings and a reduction in light waste. The highly supportive community of Newport has been vital in this regard by pushing the agenda forward in a dynamic but diplomatic fashion. Thus, by exercising patience and mobilising astute social lobbying, it is possible to influence key powerholders in initiating change. It has proved essential to earn the local community's confidence and support in order to reach the decision-makers in the early stages of developing the scheme.

The first phase of Newport's redesigned lighting plan has been delivered. From successfully applying for grant streams to organising dark sky festivals and conducting lighting tests on site, the community of Newport has shown a tremendous capacity and willpower to initiate change. Their participation in devising and installing the lighting scheme - from installing shields on lanterns to learning about how to launch a tender - has made Newport undoubtedly one of the most strategically minded communities I have worked with. As a consequence, not only has the night-time experience of the town improved, but we have also presented evidence to the county council and residents aiming to secure further dimming measures across the town, with estimated savings of 10 tonnes of CO_2 per year.

HOARE LEA (H.)

HOARE LEA

Embracing the preciousness of light, in all its forms

The Victorian artist John Atkinson Grimshaw (1836-1893) produced dramatic and creative images of cities and landscapes with natural light, artificial light and often a poetic combination of both. Famous for his nocturnal scenes, he was a pioneer in using light in all its forms to create the mood behind his canvases.

He understood that the atmosphere of a space change depends on whether it is dawn, dusk, twilight, night or day. He celebrated the transition and blend between day and night in which both work collectively to create the ambience - and employed light, shade, contrast and colour to create his final composition.

Liverpool Docks from Wapping, c.1870 by John Atkinson Grimshaw

Much like these paintings, the lighting design of spaces requires a similar appreciation. Spaces cannot simply be defined by 'day' or 'night.' They draw on a spectrum of diverse light sources - some natural, some artificial - that create the final impression. And that impression will change depending on the time of day, cloud cover, angle of the sun, seasons, weather, and atmospheric conditions.

However, when one considers the traditional disciplines of daylighting and lighting design, they often work separately with little consideration for the interaction between the light sources they use as medium for their art. It is time for closer collaboration between the two specialisms, not just to support the important aesthetic and human-centred requirements of modern spaces, but also because our planet needs us to rethink how we design to reduce the carbon footprint of the built environment.

Daylight is freely available; electric lighting consumes energy. Currently, much of this energy is generated using fossil fuels and, although the future suggests that energy can be produced from renewable sources, these will not be endless and it is incumbent on us, as designers of light, to help the world to develop a more sustainable relationship with light.

Light as a treasured luxury

Before the advent of electric lighting, we used oil lamps and candles to illuminate our spaces. As generating light involved literally burning costly resources, it was regarded as a precious commodity: light was expensive and only available to those with means. Light sources were, therefore, carried from place to place, illuminating only those tasks for which they were required. This made artificial light more personal, emphasising its value to the owner. These light sources had few components and could often be produced with insignificant impact on the general environment. Most oil lamps were ceramic and burned olive oil, beeswax or animal fats to emit light. Their components were expendable and re-usable, and there was a natural circularity in their production and operation. Although burning oil or other flammable materials is problematic in other ways, particularly in terms of air quality and fire risk, there is much to respect in our early interactions with light and light sources.

It was only with the invention of electric light bulbs and cheap energy, powered by fossil fuels, that we came to see light as an inexpensive commodity rather than a treasured luxury. We gorged on it in our homes, our workplaces and our cities. It extended our days, eliminated our nights, and redefined our sleep patterns.

Over-illuminating conversation

We did not realise the harm we were doing to ourselves, our biodiversity and our planet. We know now that extending our days and over-illuminating at night has reduced average sleep duration in the developed world and, many have argued, made us less healthy. We know that artificial light can interfere with the natural behaviour of our plant and animal species, to the extent that we must protect numerous important species from the impacts of light at night. The energy required to power our demand for electric light has led to the increased burning of fossil fuels, contributing significantly to climate change. We use elements mined from the earth, such as aluminium, plastic, copper, tantalum and yttrium to create lighting products. Some of these materials are rare, and their extraction carries social and environmental costs.

We must transform quickly if we are to meet the needs of our planet and net zero carbon commitments to address climate change. In the immediate short term, we can create more sustainable lighting by using natural and artificial light in a more connected way. By using, when available, the free resource that is daylight to illuminate spaces, and only using artificial light when it is needed, we can support wellbeing, create better spaces and reduce the energy demands of lighting systems.

The privilege that light offers

If we can redefine our relationship with light and recapture our former respect and value of artificial light, we can reduce the number of luminaires we use in projects and how much we use them. This is not to say that we need to become used to interior spaces being darker. If designers, specifiers and users could foster a greater appreciation of the privilege that light offers, we can make more conscious decisions about how we use it.

This is helped by a shift away from the old days of blanket, uniform illumination towards a desire to create spaces with different light levels, more texture and more choice. Ask anyone who works in a modern office about their lighting, and you will get a range of responses. Some people like it bright, some like it dimmer; some like daylight and others find sunlight uncomfortable. Humans are a glorious tapestry of different tastes, geographies, ages and neurotypes and the idea that we could meet everyone's needs with 500 lux and 0.6 uniformity across a workplace was always questionable. In many ways, a greater appreciation for the value of light may create a more human-centred way of designing lighting - one that better meets people's needs.

Beecroft Building, University of Oxford. Copyright Jack Hobhouse 2018

To reduce the environmental burden of artificial lighting, we need to embrace the precious value of artificial light in all its forms. This requires us, as lighting designers, to recognise daylight as the powerful light source it is and to use artificial light with greater consideration. As with all transformations, this will take time, but some of these shifts in approach can happen immediately. If we start now, we may be able to reduce some of the impacts our children face and leave a better world for their children. Humans sometimes experience natural, sometimes artificial light - and more frequently a combination of both. To be truly human-centred, we must reframe lighting design as being concerned with the overall luminous environment. Not only does this lead to more sustainable lighting, but it also provides all the wonderful benefits that natural light brings.

Blavatnik School of Government, Oxford University. Copyright John Cairns

Heathrow Terminal 2. Copyright Redshift Photography 2014

OLIVER HEATH
DESIGN

RE:MIND

Meditation and wellness centre

London UK By Oliver Heath Design

The Re:Mind store is a multi-functional meditation, healing and yoga studio set in the heart of London's bustling urban neighbourhood of Westminster. Created within an existing Victorian building, it is divided into three key spaces: a retail reception space, a recuperation community space and the meditation yoga studio. In creating and delivering the design, Oliver Heath Design took the space from being an empty masonry shell to one that considered all aspects of wellbeing, to support the physical, mental and emotional wellbeing of the occupants. To this end, a variety of biophilic design principles were introduced to enhance connections to nature in a location where it was otherwise extremely depleted.

On entering the space, visitors are welcomed by the reception and retail space offering a range of organic and natural products. Displays are created from soft, warm Douglas Fir timber; flexible rails allow for changing stock shapes and sizes. Two porthole windows offer brief glimpses into the tea-tasting areas and the meditation studio to enhance the sense of mystery and create a desire to explore the space further.

Beyond the reception area is the calming and communal recuperation space which incorporates the rehydration space. With several tea silos on the back wall of this space, Re:Mind keeps a stock of organic herbal teas and allows customers to brew and taste the teas themselves. The kitchen run is constructed from highly textural, blackened and wire-brushed timber – the heightened grain creates an absorbing, natural texture which helps to evoke a sense of nature within the space. The timber is paired with a splashback of warm pink, hand-glazed tiles and a recycled glass countertop.

OLIVER HEATH
DESIGN

A rust red, velvet banquette seat, surrounded by pot plants, sits alongside a set of timber stools which create a flexible environment for either groups or individuals in need of relaxation. While natural light from a sheltered external courtyard provides some illumination, the organic-shaped pendant lights suspended on wall brackets help to visually lower the ceiling height above the banquette, creating a comfortable, sheltered, refuge space.

The focus for Re:Mind, however, is of course the meditation space which needs to be as calming and restorative as possible, yet offer flexibility to allow for a range of wellness sessions.

The studio has two key orientations and, therefore, two focal points: the lush green planted wall and the glowing Himalayan rock-salt lamp installation. Both features frame the instructor leading the course and enhance the quality of the space in several ways.

The floor-to-ceiling green wall offers multiple benefits. Psychologically, it helps to reduce heart rates and blood pressure, while the soft reflection of light from the leaves adds visual texture, familiar fractal patterning and a wealth of restorative colour. Physiologically, it helps to filter out toxins in the air, introduces oxygen, lowers levels of CO2, moderates moisture and improves acoustics in the space.

On the opposite wall, the Himalayan rock-salt light installation within a large circular window offers a warm, natural glow. While this has been a major feature in much of the online marketing of the Re:Mind centre, the warmth, colour and texture of the rock salt lamps convey a spiritual beauty that is both calming and nurturing.

Complementing this and adding flexibility to the service offering of the space is a translucent, circular, colour-changing lighting feature set into the ceiling - ideal for chromotherapy (colour immersion therapy) sessions.

The team at Oliver Heath Design did all they could to maximise natural light in the space through the reflecting properties of paint colours, materials and features. However, proximity to the adjoining road means that the windows need to remain firmly closed to reduce traffic noise, and visual intrusion from passing buses is minimised by opaque sheer curtains and roller blinds.

Throughout the space, the use of low volatile organic compounds (VOCs) has been prioritised within materials and finishes, helping to maintain good air quality. This is supported by a HEPA filter air-filtration system to improve indoor air quality, which can be affected by the urban setting outside the space.

It is evident from the design, the way it is used, and the feedback received that clients and staff alike feel a deep connection to the healing qualities of the space. The multi-sensory approach creates a layered experience that helps to reduce stress and aids mental and physical recuperation in a way that feels intuitive and natural - all qualities that biophilic design aspires to deliver.

OLIVER HEATH
DESIGN

FRANKIE BOYLE STUDIO

A Trailblazing Lighting Artist.

In the realm of contemporary art, few shine as brightly as Frankie Boyle, a trailblazing lighting artist whose innovative work has redefined the boundaries of perception and human experience. Through her unique focus on light as a medium to communicate and influence human movement, Boyle has harnessed the very essence of electromagnetic waves to create transformative art that resonates deeply with the human psyche.

Light, as Boyle passionately asserts, is not merely a utilitarian tool that illuminates our surroundings; it is a dynamic wavelength that engages with our senses on a profound level. Embedded within the intricate neural pathways of our brains, light triggers a cascade of emotions, memories and physiological responses. Boyle's journey into the captivating world of lighting art began through curiosity - a desire to explore how these wavelengths could be harnessed to evoke emotions, alter perceptions and, ultimately, transform states of being.

Frankie's artistic process is a meticulous fusion of scientific inquiry and creative expression. With an unwavering commitment to understanding the intricate interplay between light and the human mind, she delves into the physics of wavelengths, colour theory and the psychology of perception. Armed with this knowledge, she becomes an alchemist of light, concocting mesmerising installations that take viewers on immersive journeys of self-discovery.

In one of Boyle's most celebrated works, The Living Lantern, an outdoor installation nestled in an urban park, she ingeniously employs light as a catalyst for communal interactions. As the sun dips below the horizon, Boyle's installation awakens, casting ever-changing hues across the landscape. Families gather, friends converse and strangers connect as they are bathed in its captivating radiance. The shared experience becomes a symphony of human connection, orchestrated by the harmonious wavelengths of light in connection with the kinetic membrane triggered by mother nature.

Lucid is a testament to Boyle's mastery over light's emotive power. In a vast, dimly lit gallery, suspended luminescent threads hang like tendrils of possibility, their soft, pulsating glow inviting visitors to step into a realm of altered consciousness. As spectators venture deeper into the installation, the interplay of light and shadow gently guides their movements, creating an ethereal dance between humans and illumination. The neurological responses to these shifting wavelengths are undeniable – heart rates synchronise with the rhythm of the light, breathing patterns shift and a palpable sense of tranquillity envelops all who enter.

While Boyle's art is undeniably captivating, it is the intention behind each creation that lends her work an enduring impact. She ardently believes that the emotional and psychological responses elicited by her installations hold the key to unlocking latent aspects of human consciousness. Through a controlled manipulation of wavelengths of light, Boyle seeks to guide viewers into states of introspection, mindfulness and even euphoria. Hers is an artistic endeavour driven by an unwavering belief in light's capacity to elevate the human experience.

In a world inundated with sensory distractions and digital detachment, Boyle's lighting art offers a poignant reminder of the profound connection we share with the natural world and the universe at large. Her creations are a conduit through which individuals can rekindle their innate relationship with light, basking in its radiance and surrendering to its transformative embrace.

As Frankie Boyle continues to explore the frontiers of lighting art, her dedication to unravelling the intricate dance between light and human consciousness remains constant. Through her masterful manipulation of wavelengths, she not only creates visually stunning installations but also taps into the very essence of what it means to be human. With each stroke of her artistic brush, Boyle invites us to journey into the luminous tapestry of our own minds, where light is not just an external force, but a profound catalyst for metamorphosis - an eternal wavelength that shapes and reshapes the contours of our existence.

SECTION 5

Phos –
Sustainable, biophilic lighting instruments

PROJECT: MAYFAIR PARK RESIDENCES
LIGHTING DESIGNER: ISOMETRIX

ENRICHING
MINDS, SPACES
AND HABITATS
- OUR VISION

Marriot Autograph Hotel | UAE
Lighting Designer: Smith Tait
Sindalah Island

MULTI-AWARD-WINNING MANUFACTURER

Phos is a British architectural lighting manufacturer specialising in crafting highly modular and precision-engineered light instruments. These can be designed before and after installation down to the very last detail. Based in Hertfordshire, England, the company has been family-owned since 1883, spanning 5 generations and has a history of excellence in British engineering, manufacturing 90% of our components locally to this day.

We believe there can be no compromise when it comes to aesthetics, functionality, sustainability, and quality and are proud to offer industry-leading light quality, unrivalled finishing options and a full biophilic business structure. This ethos has won us awards from some of the most respected institutions in the lighting design sector as well as the British monarchy, receiving the coveted King's Award, making us one of the top British manufacturers based on international performance and company standards.

With a comprehensive range of products and solutions that cater to the residential, commercial, marine and hospitality sectors, Phos is available in over 40 countries, across five continents and our products are used in some of the most prestigious projects in the world.

[d]arc awards WINNER 2019
[d]arc awards 2ND PLACE 2020
[d]arc awards WINNER 2021
[d]arc awards WINNER 2022
[d]arc awards 2023 SHORTLISTED

FX International Design Awards SHORTLIST 2020
LIGHTING DESIGN AWARDS 2020 HIGHLY COMMENDED
FX International Design Awards SHORTLIST 2021
THE INTERNATIONAL DESIGN & ARCHITECTURE AWARDS
The King's Awards for Enterprise International Trade 2024

THE KING'S AWARDS FOR ENTERPRISE

INTERNATIONAL TRADE

2024

KING'S AWARD FOR ENTERPRISE

Phos is honoured to be recognised as a recipient of the prestigious King's Award for Enterprise, an esteemed accolade celebrating outstanding achievement by UK businesses. Formerly known as The Queen's Award for Enterprise, this programme acknowledges organisations that excel in areas such as international trade, innovation, sustainable development, and promoting opportunity. It stands as the highest official UK award for British businesses.

This recognition is testament to our commitment to innovation and international trade. Over the past three years (2021-2024), Phos has experienced remarkable growth in overseas sales, with a 240% increase in international trade making up 33% of total sales.

Receiving this award underlines the hard work and dedication of our team, as well as the support of our partners and customers worldwide. We are incredibly proud of this achievement and remain committed to driving further innovation and excellence in all aspects of our business.

ENGINEERING HERITAGE

1883 Swiss national, Richard Cadisch arrives in the UK and starts, R.Cadisch & Sons - supplying household equipment and operating from London

1930s R.Cadisch and Sons venture into the electrical wholesale market

1960s The motor and household equipment companies are sold, and a new industrial filtration business, Cadisch Precision Meshes, is formed

1900s The motor trade business is formed, manufacturing motor accessories and garage equipment

1950s R.Cadisch & Sons is awarded 2 Royal Warrants as suppliers of household equipment to the royal family. Now also a household name and one of the leading motor accessories businesses in the country

2000s Cadisch Metal for Design and Architecture (MDA) is formed, going on to become one of the leading producers of architectural and decorative metals

2022 Five generations later, multiple awards and a huge number of globally registered patents, Phos is internationally recognised and has distribution networks that spans the world

disch Precision shes is awarded a ntract to supply filters the aeronautical gines of Rolls Royce

2009 The group moves into the architectural lighting sector forming LED company Ecoled, leaning on it's rich heritage in engineering and finishes

2019 Ecoled goes through rebranding exercise and becomes, Phos

Today Phos receives the prestigious King's Award for Enterprise, the highest official UK award for British businesses with a 240% increase in international trade making up 33% of total sales

WHY PHOS?

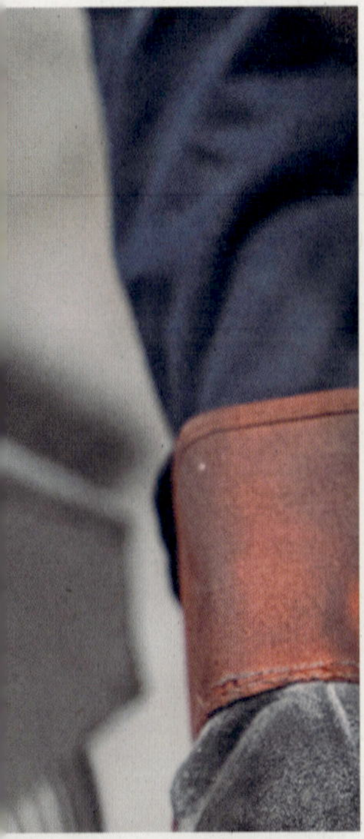

140 YEARS OF
SUSTAINABLE BRITISH
ENGINEERING

UNRIVALLED FLAWLESS
FINISHES

MODULAR AND NATURAL
ILLUMINATION

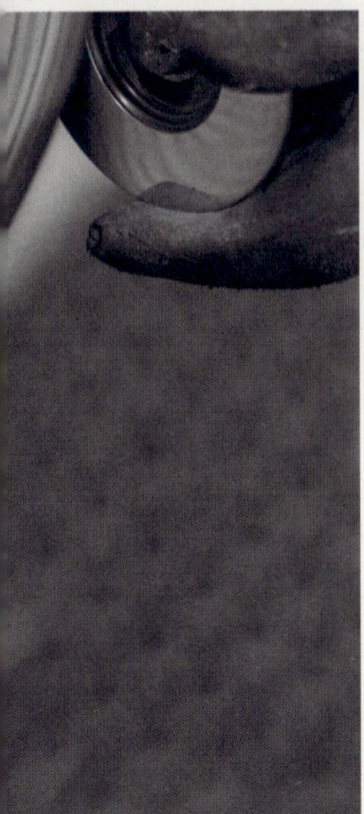

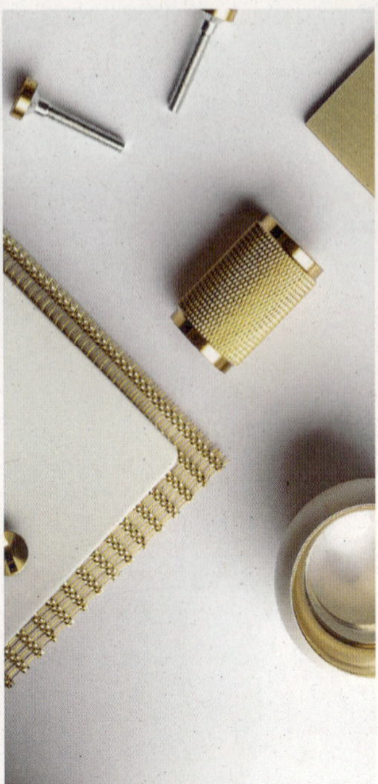

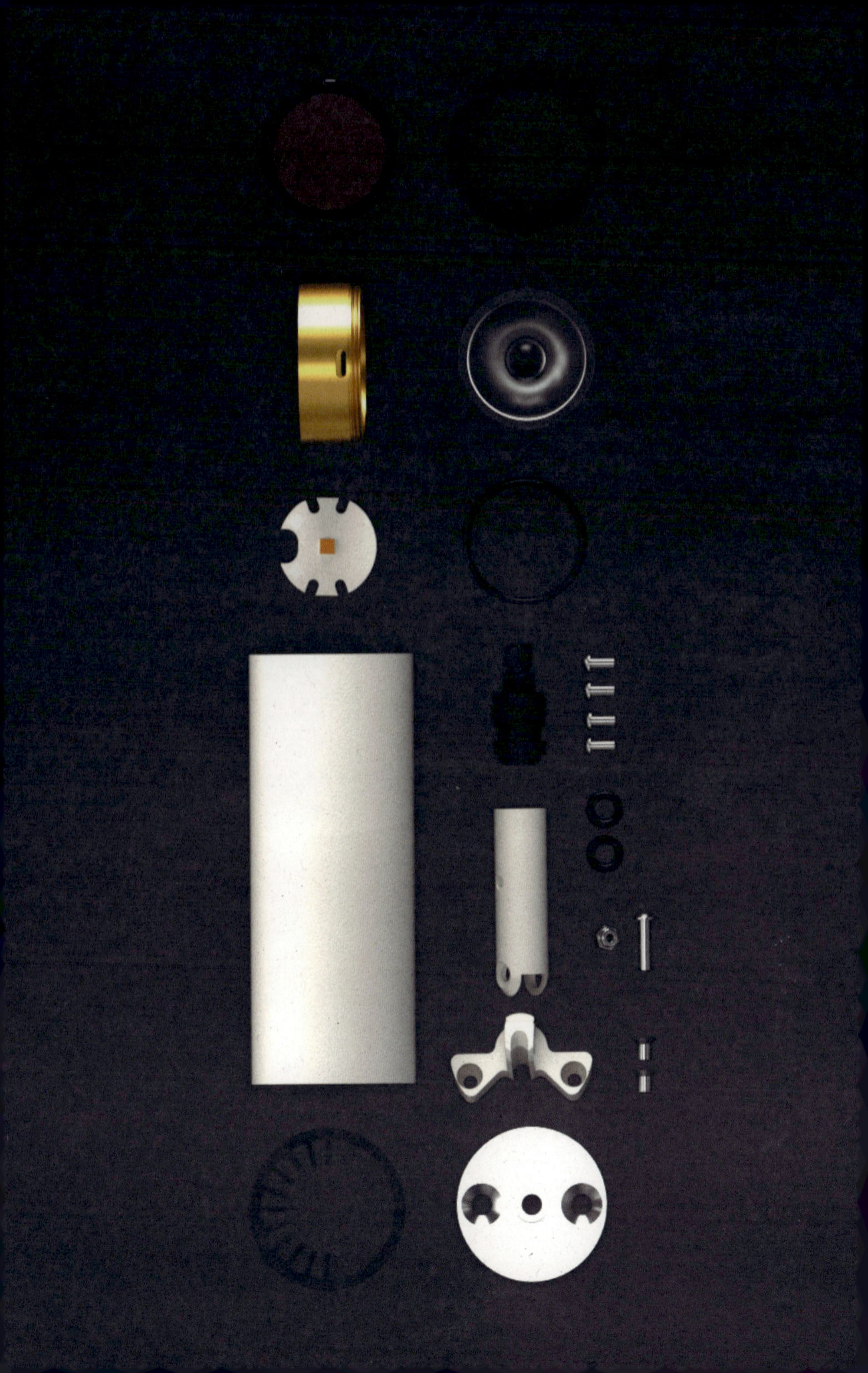

CIRCULAR
REGEN
Regeneration for Generations

LIFETIME PROJECT SUPPORT

We are highly committed to environmentally friendly practices and the principles of a circular economy, prioritising an **unlimited duty of care** for all our manufactured components. This ensures that we repair, reuse, recycle, and ReGenerate everything we manufacture to conserve vital resources.

We encourage all fixtures to be returned to us so we can ReGen or recycle.

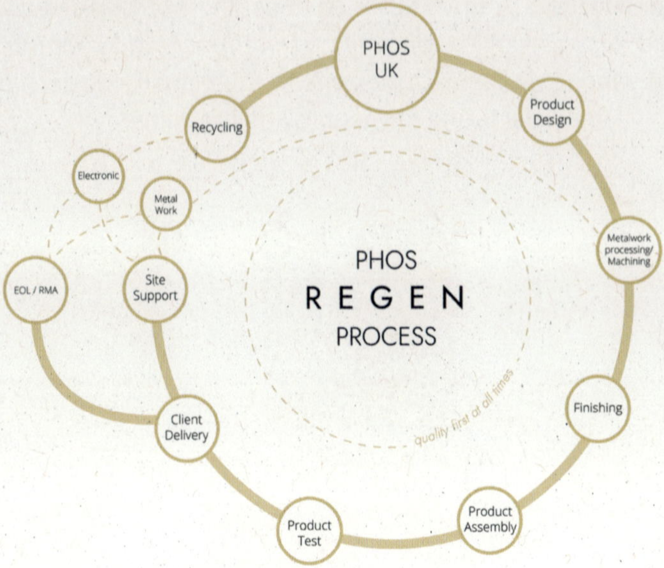

Learn More

B CORP ACCREDITATION

B Corp assesses a company's social and environmental impact as well as their ethics and transparency. At the time of writing this, we are one of only two companies with B Corp accreditation in the architectural lighting sector.

This means that the Phos ethos has been fully scrutinised and awarded this challenging piece of certification. With it, our multi-award-winning range becomes one of the industry leaders in manufacturing for people and for planet.

Learn More

Certified
B
Corporation

PHOS
PHOS

PHOS DRIVERS

Marine Plastic Waste

We use ocean-bound plastic to manufacture our LED drivers. By repurposing marine plastic waste, we combat plastic pollution and reduce demand for new plastic production. All part of our B Corp and circular economy goals.

Flicker-Free

•All Phos drivers (1% mains, 0-10V / 0.1% DALI) dim to 1 or 0.1%.
•EE1789 compliant, meaning they are optimal for human health and wellness.
•Auto cut-out and auto recover enabled.
•Auto cut-out when overheated and overloaded.
•Analogue flicker-free.

Flicker Document

Sustainability Document

PHOS IS FULLY OFF-GRID

We are fully off-grid, meaning that all electricity used on our premises comes from natural solar power. We even have enough left over to contribute back to our local community via the national grid.

Learn More

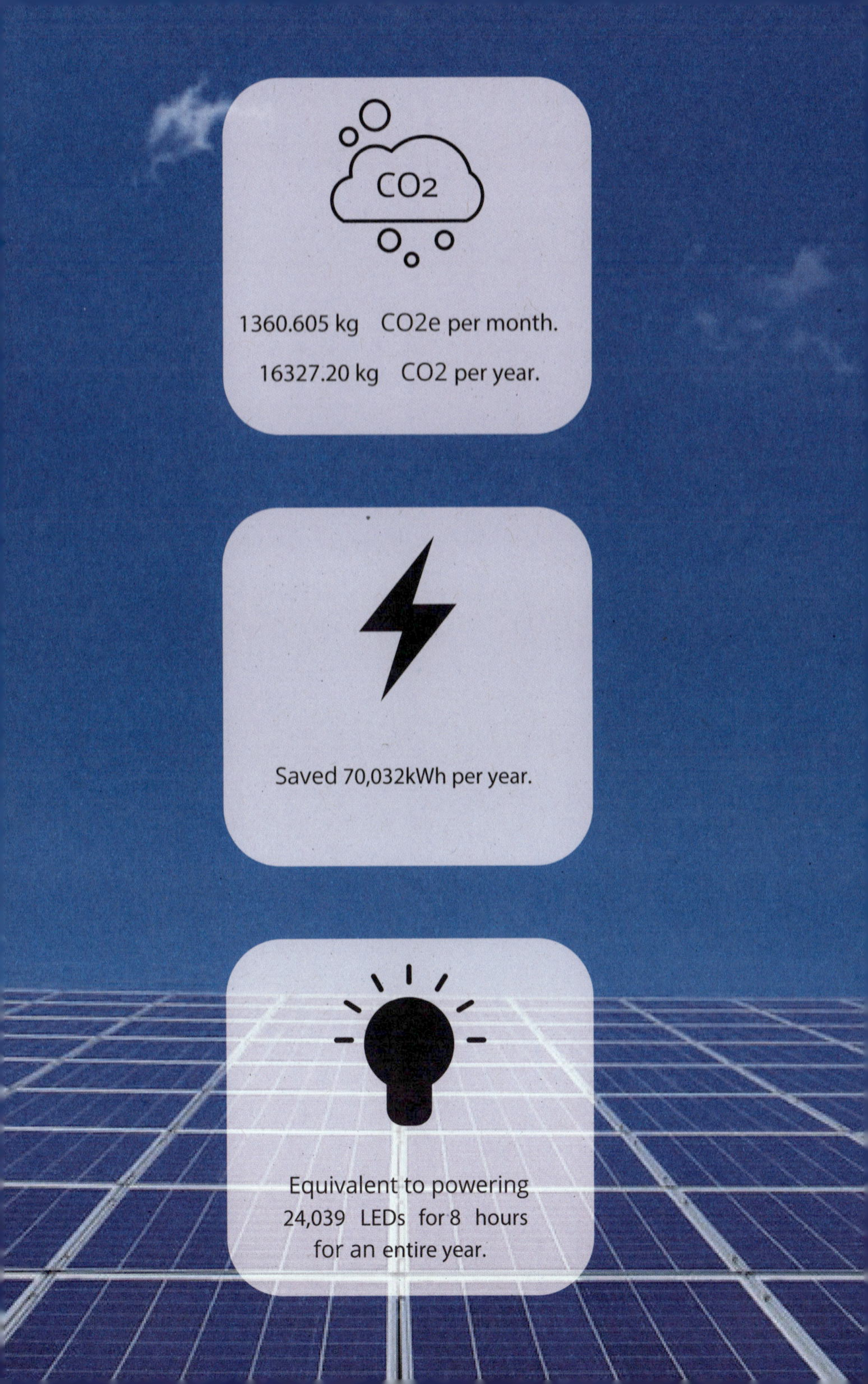
CO2
1360.605 kg CO2e per month.
16327.20 kg CO2 per year.
Saved 70,032kWh per year.
Equivalent to powering
24,039 LEDs for 8 hours
for an entire year.

RECYCLABILITY OF PHOS PRODUCT

:Compontents that are recycled

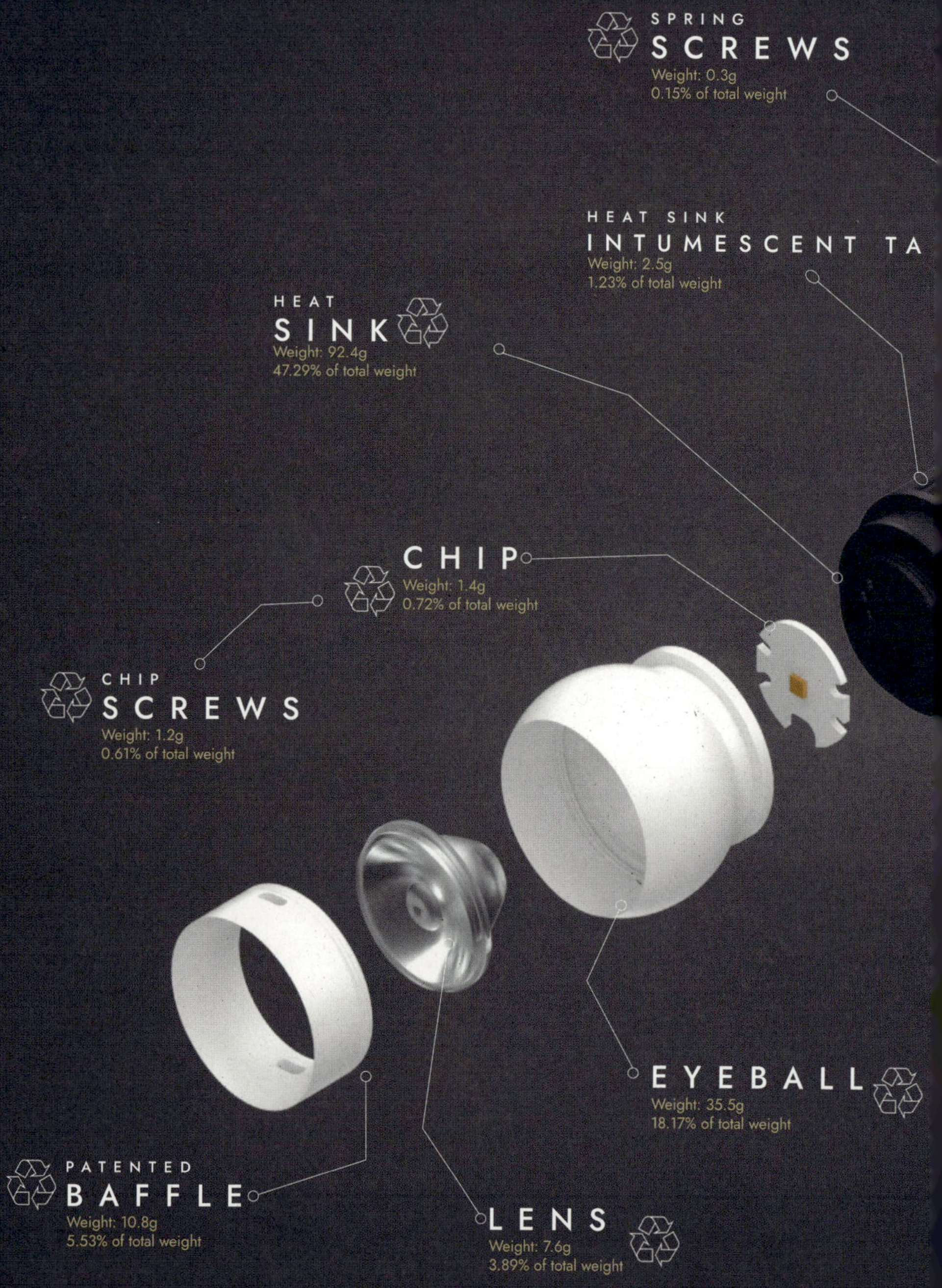

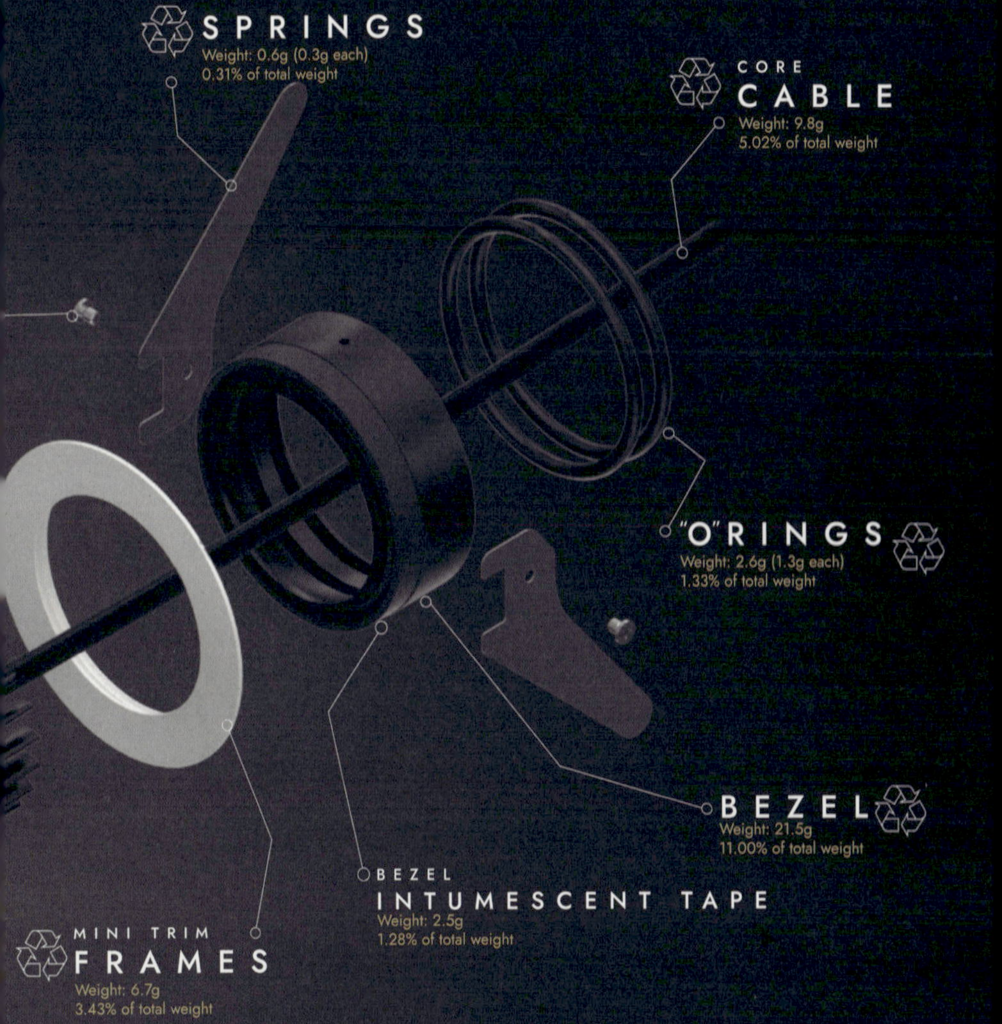

TOTAL:

Weight: 213.5g

97.45% of product recyclable

PHOS
ENGINEERING

PACKAGING

We only use recyclable and environmentally friendly packaging (primarily cardboard). We turn all incoming cardboard and paper into protective packaging for outgoing goods, using a specialist shredding machine.

Our specially designed packaging uses recyclable sealant tape that's water-based meaning no harmful glues touch the boxes we ship.

Learn More

TM65

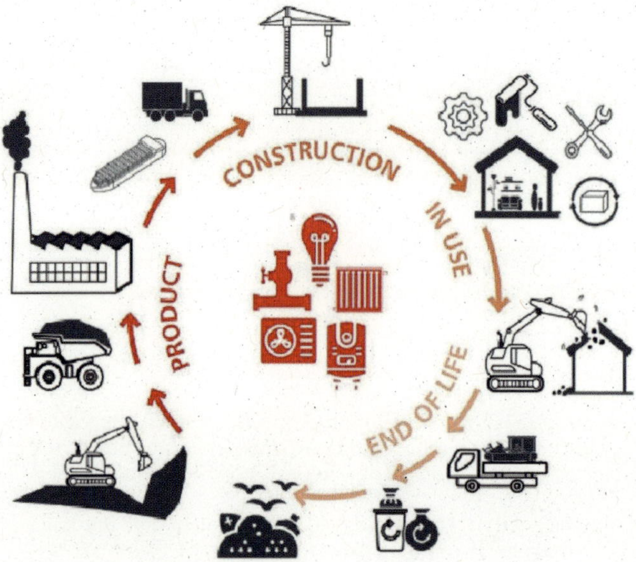

CIBSE has developed the TM65 standard methodology for the assessment of embodied carbon so embodied carbon data calculated by different consultants and researchers can be brought together, compared, and 'rules of thumb' developed for embodied carbon of MEP systems.

To make this possible, CIBSE encourages users of TM65 to submit calculation results to CIBSE using a standard reporting form, together with the form submitted by a product's manufacturer.

Available on Request

TM66

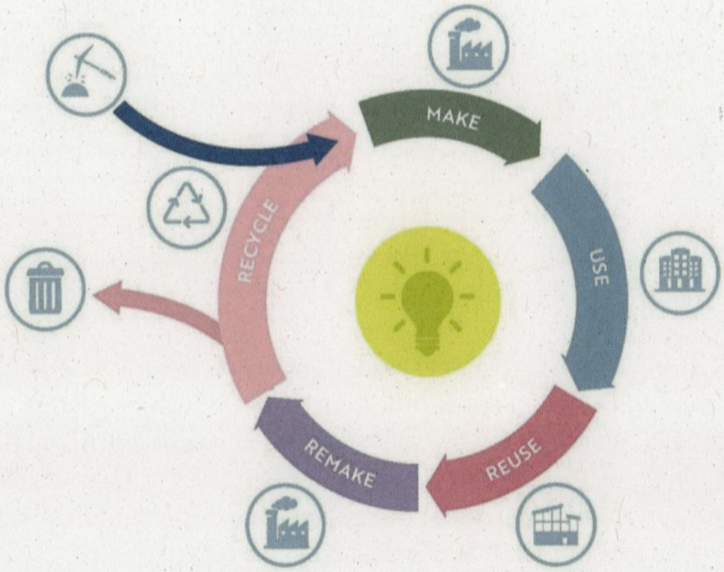

Creating a circular economy in the lighting industry.

The aim of TM66 is to drive the move to sustainable futures. We must all assess and report on not just our commercial performance, but our environmental impact. The increasingly visible effects of man-made climate change, the COP26 conference and the questions over energy and resource scarcity have made the move towards a Circular Economy never more relevant than now.

The answer is all about design, not just product design, but the design of an eco-system of scheme design, facilities management and supporting services that keep products delivering value for the longest period of time.

See Full Report

WEEE RECYCLED

Phos has WEEE compliant certification, meaning we design our products with environmentally-safe recycling and recovery in mind.

Any products that cannot be repaired are designed for deconstruction and are responsibly recycled.

Learn More

WEEE Compliant

R. CADISCH & SONS
THE RELIABLE WHOLESALERS
ONDON & BRANCHES
1934-35
CATALOGUE No. 116
PARTS.
OLS AND
EQUIPMENT

reewild

Phos proudly partners with Reewild. With their help, we removed our carbon emissions with a portfolio of best-in-class carbon removal projects, from UK-based afforestation to overseas renewable energy credits.

So far phos has removed 76 tonnes of CO_2e, this is the equivalent of 56 flights, or 186,000 miles driven, or even 9,566,326 phones charged.

This is all part of our plan to become net zero by 2030.

GreenLight Alliance

Phos is a proud member of the Green Light Alliance, whose aim is to light up the world, without depleting its resources.

Made up of an alliance of suppliers, specifiers, and educators, we aim to shape the debate around sustainable lighting and make a difference to the world in which we live.

Recolight

Reuse | Recycle.

Phos is a proud member of Recolight. With their support, we're able to effectively stay ahead of the curve on all matters of sustainability.

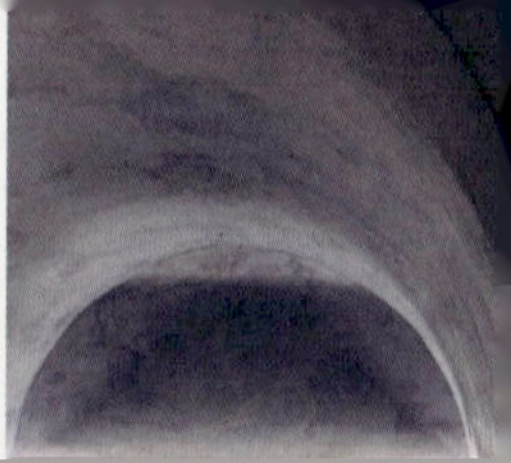

RESIDENTIAL | SHENFIELD MILL
PHOTOGRAPHY: IQ GLASS

PROJECTS

The Phos product ranges have been chosen by designers around the world to illuminate some of the finest residential, hospitality, marine and commercial spaces in the market today.

Learn More

HOSPITALITY | MANDARIN ORIENTAL HOTEL | MAYFAIR
LIGHTING DESIGNER: DPA | ARCHITECT: CLIVEDALE

COMMERCIAL | 73 BROOK STREET
INTERIOR DESIGNER: STUDIO INDIGO | ARCHITECT: PLP ARCHITECTURE

You can
Brew it

MARINE | GALAXY SUPER YACHT

PRODUCT MODULARITY

PRODUCT MODULARITY

POWER OPTIONS

All our lights come in various wattage and size options – **Nano, Standard and Maxi.**

SOCKET OPTIONS

Phos products feature a patented system in **fixed, adjustable, or wall wash** options.

FLAWLESS FINISHING

Phos offer an **unrivalled** palette of finishing options or can machine specific metal alloys on every component we make.

INNER BAFFLE

All Phos products feature a **patented interchangeable baffle system** that allows for easy customisation and flexibility in design.

LIGHT ENGINES

A range of different LED chip options are available - **Standard** (90 CRI), **Dim to Warm** (95 CRI), **Genesis** (98 CRI), **Genesis Tuneable White** (98 CRI), and a **High Efficiency** (90 CRI) chip. All available in 2700k, 3000k and 4000k

BEAM ANGLES

Our optics are completely interchangeable, both **before** and **after** installation, and come in **10°, 20°, 30°, 40°, and 50°** options.

ACCESSORIES

Phos offers a range of interchangeable accessories that can be added or changed post-installation, housed in a recessed or flush holder. These accessories include **elliptical lenses, softening lenses, colour filters, and honeycomb louvres,** (up to 3 accessories per holder).

FRAME OPTIONS

A huge range of frame / installation options are available, including **mini trims, squares, recessed, trimless, twins, and triples.**

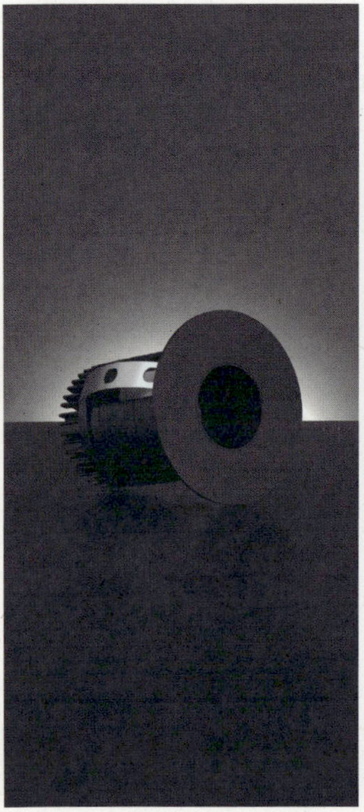
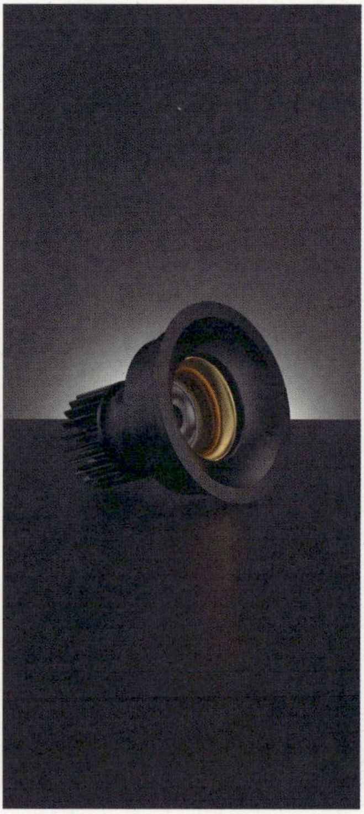
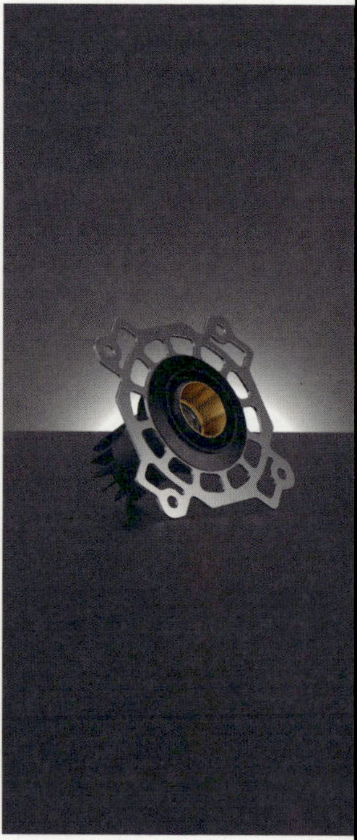

STANDARD WHITE
90CRI
HIGH EFFICENCY
90CRI
LED CHIP OPTIONS · LED CHIP OPTIONS ·
GENESIS /
GENESIS TUNEABLE
98CRI
DIM TO WARM
90CRI

INDUSTRY-LEADING LIGHT QUALITY

Fixed and tuneable light engines that offer the closest thing to natural light.

90CRI as standard with option to upgrade to our Dim-to-Warm (90 CRI), Genesis (98CRI) and Genesis Tuneable LEDs (98CRI) lifting the colour and vibrancy in your space like no other.

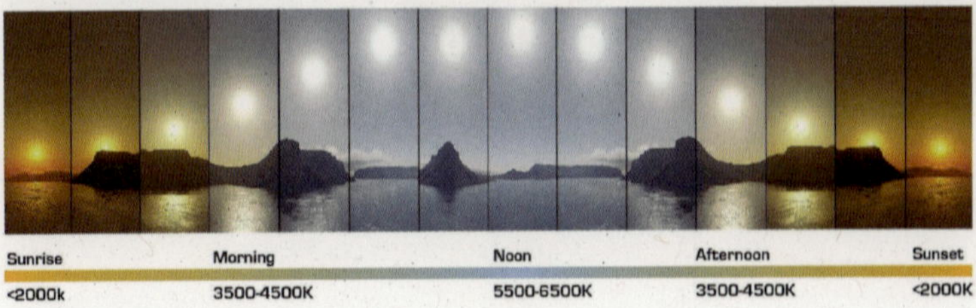

INDUSTRY - LEADING
FLAWLESS FINISHES

PLATED

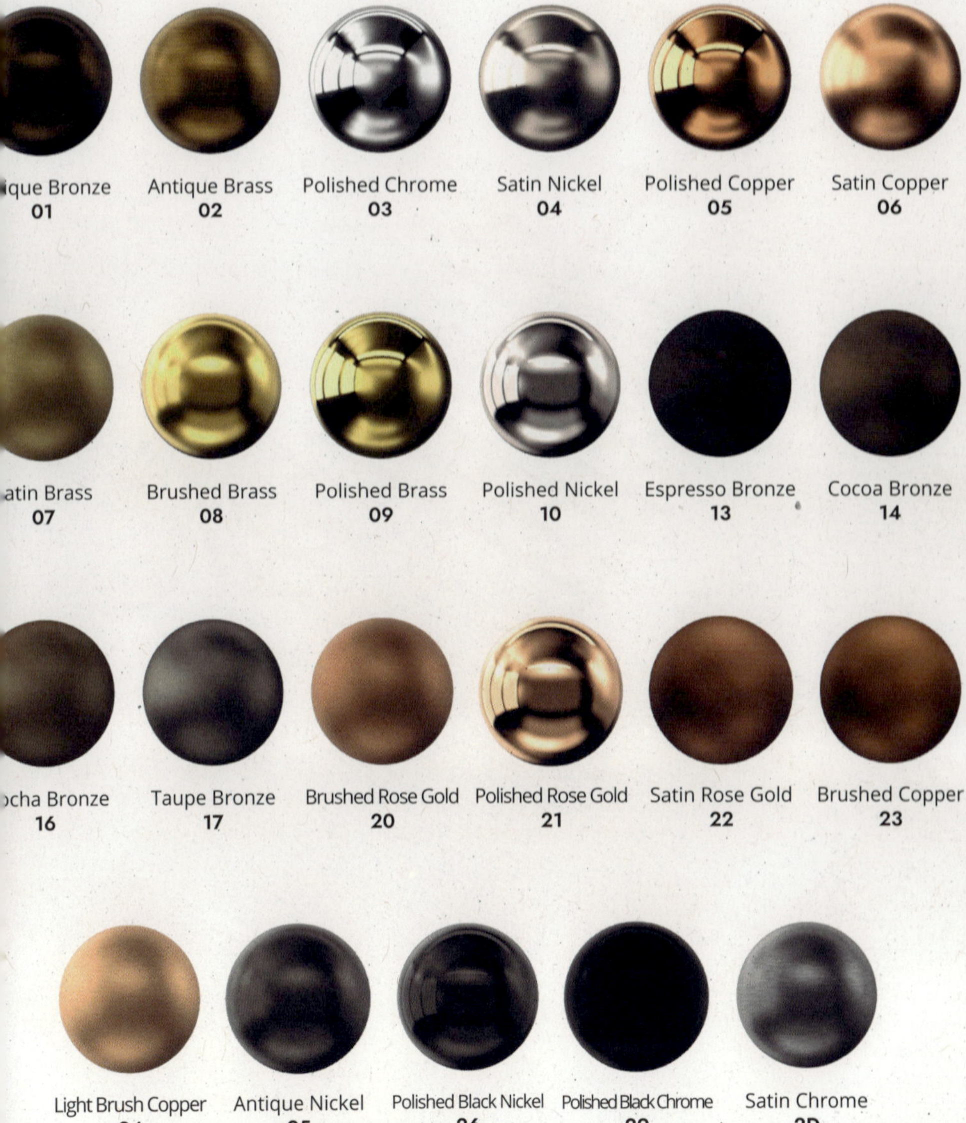

ique Bronze
01
Antique Brass
02
Polished Chrome
03
Satin Nickel
04
Polished Copper
05
Satin Copper
06
atin Brass
07
Brushed Brass
08
Polished Brass
09
Polished Nickel
10
Espresso Bronze
13
Cocoa Bronze
14
cha Bronze
16
Taupe Bronze
17
Brushed Rose Gold
20
Polished Rose Gold
21
Satin Rose Gold
22
Brushed Copper
23
Light Brush Copper
24
Antique Nickel
25
Polished Black Nickel
26
Polished Black Chrome
29
Satin Chrome
2D

ALMALEATHER

ANODISED

Tuba Brass
11

Antique Gold
12

Ice Gold
15

24K Gold
18

Champagne Gold
19

Anodised Black
B1

POWDER COATED

Primed
00

Satin Jet Black
B2

Matte Jet Black
B3

Black Textured
BT

White Textured
WT

RAL Classic
(any colour available)

RAL Design
(any colour available)

MARINE-GRADE & METAL POWDER COATED

MARINE-GRADE

Raw Copper
2X

Raw Brass
2Y

Raw Bronze
2Z

METAL POWDER COAT

Cocoa Bronze
J1

Antique Brass
K1

Mocha Bronze
KD

SPECIALIST FINISHES

POWDER COAT

Sandstone
SDS

Concrete
CON

Rust
RST

Limestone
LES

PLATED

Oxidised Copper
2A

Oxidised Brass
2B

THE HILTON | BATH

BIOPHILIC DESIGN

Biophilic. *noun – "An innate and genetically determined affinity of human beings with the natural world."*

Driven by the local community, naturally occurring shapes, colours and textures, full-spectrum light and respect for the planet, Phos fittings are some of the most biophilic on the planet. With LED chips that most closely replicate that of the visible light spectrum, natural finishes (such as sandstone, limestone and rust) found only in nature and biomorphic shapes and mechanisms in our products, choosing Phos means choosing a reconnection to the natural world.

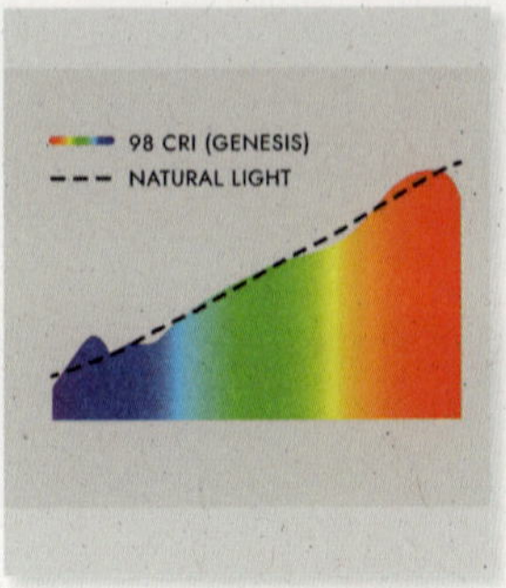

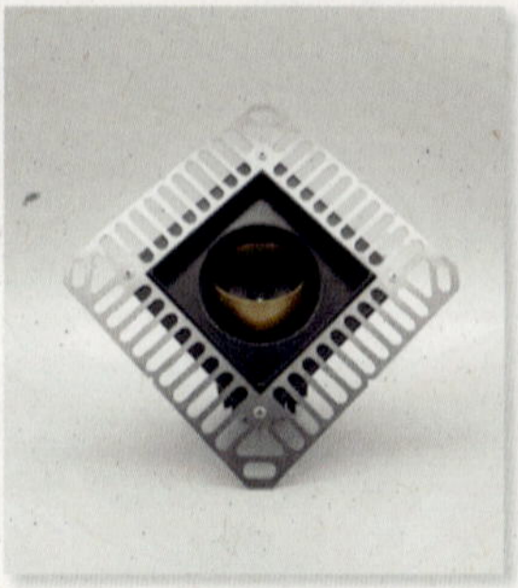

Follow QR code to watch our biophilic manufacturing video

Follow QR code to watch our sustainable manufacturing video

DISTRIBUTION NETWORK

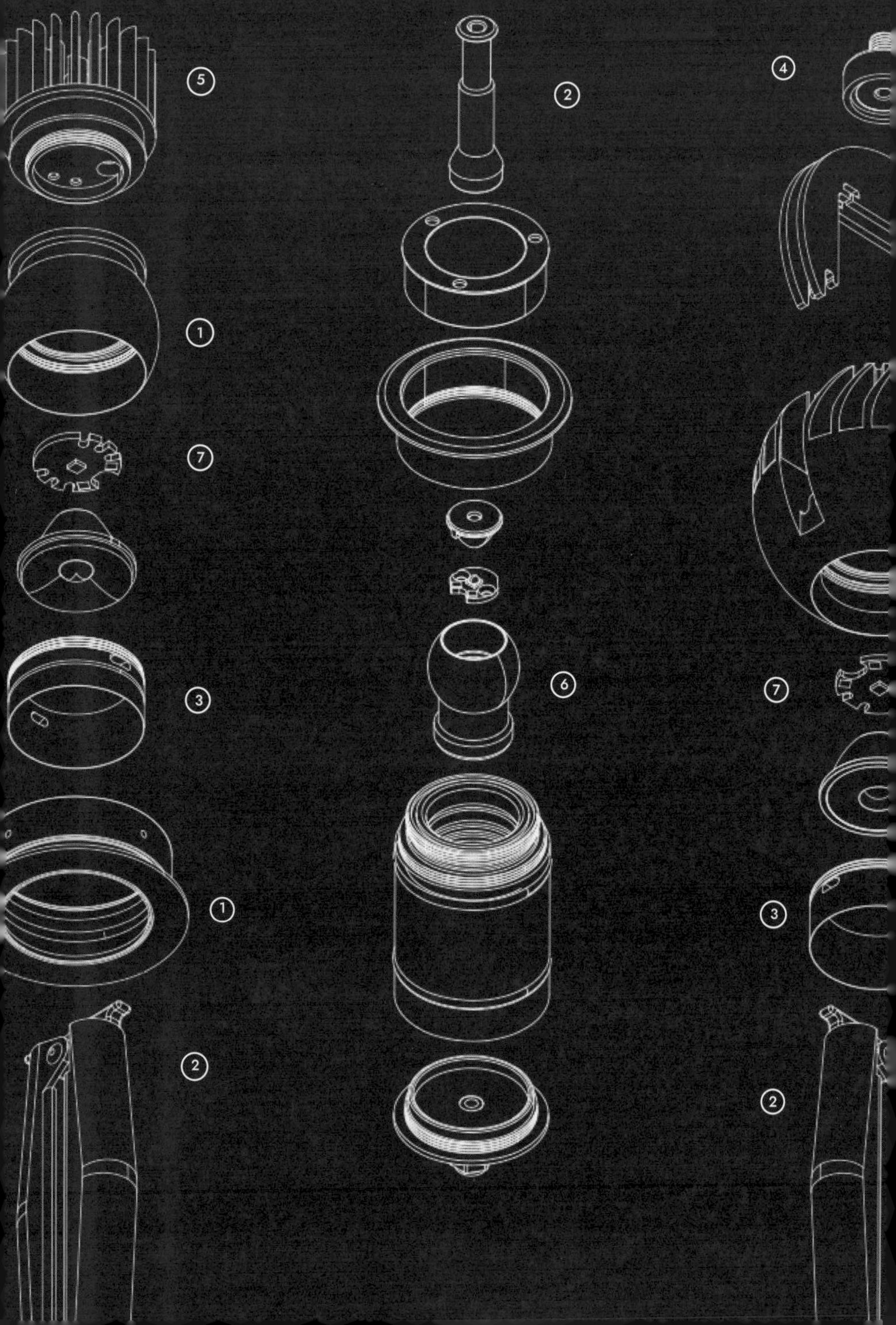
5
2
4
1
7
6
7
3
1
3
2
2

DESIGN PATENTS

For over a century, Phos has passionately strived for engineering excellence. Our multi-award-winning luminaires are a result of this longstanding drive to innovate materials, technology, and products. These unique and cutting-edge designs have resulted in seven patents (and counting!)

1. EYEBALL & SOCKET JOINT
2. BEAM TARGETTING COMMISSIONING TOOL
3. INTERCHANGABLE BEZEL, BAFFLE AND LENS
4. ORBA MAGNETIC COUPLING MECHANISM
5. TWO-PART HEATSINK FORGING
6. INGROUND ADJUSTABLE SOCKET JOINT
7. LED/PCB HEAT DISSIPATION SYSTEM

ACCREDITATION & CERTIFICATION

RoHS
Restriction of Hazardous substance

Flexitime Hours
Allowing employees to alter workday start and finish times

RED
Restriction of harmful materials to living creatures

REACH
Restriction of Chemicals

BCORP
Verification of social & environmental performance

Fair Living Wage
Allowing employees to afford a decent standard of living

WEEE
Waste Electrical and Electronic Equipment recycling

Ecologi
Sponsoring carbon offsetting

TM66
Adopting the Circular Economy in the Lighting Industry

Packaging
Recycling and Environmentally friendly

Community Impact
Sponsoring and collaborating with local organisations e.g. Hertfordshire University

Surfers Against Sewage
Marine conservation charity working with communities to protect oceans, beaches and marine life

Mayfair Mews House. Designer: Maxwell Barlow

Appendices

References

Section 1: What is biophilic design?

1. Fromm, E. (1973). The Anatomy of Human Destructiveness. New York, Holt, Rinehart and Winston.

2. Wilson, E.O. (1984) Biophilia. Harvard University Press.

3. S. Kellert, J.H. Heerwagen, and M.L. Mador (eds) (2008). Biophilic Design: The Theory, Science & Practice of Bringing Buildings to Life. John Wiley & Sons, Hoboken, NJ.

4. Browning, W., & Ryan, C. (2020). Nature Inside: A Biophilic Design Guide. Taylor & Francis, Oxfordshire, UK. doi: 10.4324/9781003033011.

5. Brynie, F.H. (2009). Brain sense: the science of the senses and how we process the world around us. Amacom, USA.

6. Macruz, A., Bueno, E., Palma, G.G., Vega, J., Palmieri, R.A., Wu, T.C. (2022). Measuring Human Perception of Biophilically-Driven Design with Facial Micro-expressions Analysis and EEG Biosensor. In: Yuan, P.F., Chai, H., Yan, C., Leach, N. (eds) Proceedings of the 2021 DigitalFUTURES. CDRF 2021. Springer, Singapore. https://doi.org/10.1007/978-981-16-5983-6_22

7. Marshall, T. (2022). 'People and Nature Survey: How has COVID-19 changed how we engage with nature?' Available at: https://naturalengland.blog.gov.uk/2022/05/18/people-and-nature-survey-how-has-covid-19-changed-the-way-we-engage-with-nature/ (Accessed 08/11/22).

8. Hillman, E.M. (2007). Optical brain imaging in vivo: techniques and applications from animal to man. J Biomed Opt. 12(5):051402. doi: 10.1117/1.2789693. PMID: 17994863; PMCID: PMC2435254.

9. Voss, B. (1996). The Journal of Business Strategy, 17(2), p.62.

10. Becker F.D., and Lynn, M.L. (1986). The importance of office closure versus quality in job selection. In J. Wineman, R Barnes, C. Zimring (eds). Proceedings of the Environmental Design Research Association. The Costs of Not Knowing. EDRA 17. Atlanta, GA: Environmental Design Research Association.

11. Lohr, V., Pearson-Mims, C., and Goodwin, G. (1995). Interior Plants May Improve Worker Productivity and Reduce Stress in a Windowless Environment. Environ. Hort. 14. doi: 10.24266/0738-2898-14.2.97.

12. Ulrich, R.S. (1993). Biophilia, biophobia, and natural landscapes. The biophilia hypothesis, 7, pp.73-137.

13. Ulrich, R.S. (1984). View through a window may influence recovery from surgery. Science, 224(4647), pp.420-421.

14. Elzeyadi, I. (2011). Daylighting-bias and biophilia: quantifying the impact of daylighting on occupants' health. US Green Building Council. http://www.usgbc.org/sites/default/files/OR10_Daylighting% 20Bias% 20and% 20Biophilia. pdf.

15. Makes. N.I.M. and Sense. F., 2012. The economics of biophilia.
16. Heschong, L. (1999). Daylighting in Schools: An Investigation into the Relationship Between Daylighting and Human Performance. Condensed report. 10.13140/RG.2.2.31498.31683.

17. Kahn, P. H., Severson, R. L., & Ruckert, J. H. (2009). The Human Relation With Nature and Technological Nature. Current Directions in Psychological Science, 18(1), 37-42. https://doi.org/10.1111/j.1467-8721.2009.01602.x

18. Browning, W.D. and Ryan, C.O., 2020. Nature inside: a biophilic design guide. Routledge.

19. Geddes, L. (2019). Chasing the Sun. Simon and Schuster.

20. McLeod, J., 2016. Colour Psychology Today. John Hunt Publishing.

21. Lee, S. and Kim, Y. (2021). A framework of biophilic urbanism for improving climate change adaptability in urban environments. Urban Forestry & Urban Greening, 61, p.127104.

22. Skolny, C.A. (2008). The effect of classroom lighting on the volume of classroom sounds. West Virginia University.

23. US Dept of Health and Human Services, National Hospital Discharge Survey, 2010 / Terrapin.

24. Loftness, V. (2008). Sustainable Design for Health and Productivity,

25. Stroebele, N., and De Castro, J.M. (2004). Effect of ambience on food intake and food choice. Nutrition, 20(9), pp.821-838.

Section 2: How we see and connect to the world around us

1. Kanazawa, S. (2004). The savanna principle. Managerial and decision economics, 25(1), pp.41-54.

2. Xu, K. (2019). A long journey of lithium: from the big bang to our smartphones. Energy & Environmental Materials, 2(4), pp.229-233.

3. Geddes, L. (2019). Chasing the Sun. Simon and Schuster.

4. Schopf, J.W. (2012). The fossil record of cyanobacteria. In Ecology of cyanobacteria II (pp.15-36). Springer, Dordrecht.

5. Ameisen, J.C. (2002). On the origin, evolution, and nature of programmed cell death: a four billion-year timeline. Cell Death & Differentiation, 9(4), pp.367-393.

6. Schwab, I.R. (2011). Evolution's witness: how eyes evolved. Oxford University Press.

7. Fernald, R.D. (2000). Evolution of eyes. Current opinion in neurobiology, 10(4), pp.444-450.

8. Bryson, B. (2004). A short history of nearly everything. Broadway.

9. Wilcox, C. (2012). Evolution: Out Of The Sea. Available at: https://blogs.scientificamerican.com/science-sushi/evolution-out-of-the-sea/. (Accessed on: 9 November 2022).

10. Hall, B.K. (2005). Bones and cartilage: developmental and evolutionary skeletal biology. Elsevier.

11. Bryson, B. (2019). The body: a guide for occupants. First United States edition. New York, Doubleday.

12. D'Elia, K.P., and Dasen, J.S. (2018). Development, functional organization, and evolution of vertebrate axial motor circuits. Neural development, 13(1), pp.1-12.

13. Lamb, T.D. (2011). Evolution of the eye. Scientific American, 305(1), pp.64-69.

14. Yoto, A., Katsuura, T., Iwanaga, K., and Shimomura, Y. (2007). Effects of object color stimuli on human brain activities in perception and attention referred to EEG alpha band response. Journal of physiological anthropology, 26(3), pp.373-379.

15. Ross, M.J., Guthrie, P. and Dumont, J.C. (2013). The impact of modulated color light on the autonomic nervous system. Adv Mind-Body Med, 27(4), pp.7-16.

16. Haller, K. (2019). The Little Book of Colour. Penguin.

17. Dessoir, M. (1892). Über den Hautsinn. Arch. f. Anat. u. Physiol., Physiol. Abt., 175-339.

18. Gregory, R.L. (1989). Light on black boxes. Perception, 18(3), pp.281-284.

19. National Center for Biotechnology Information. 'Why Is There So Much More Research on Vision Than on Any Other Sensory Modality?'. https://www.ncbi.nlm.nih.gov/pmc/articles/PMC6787282/.(Accessed 10 November 2022)

20. Köhler, W. (1929). An old pseudoproblem. Naturwissenschaften, 17, pp.395-401.

21. Fort, M., Martin, A., and Peperkamp, S. (2015). Consonants are more important than vowels in the bouba-kiki effect. Language and Speech, 58(2), pp.247-266.

22. Ćwiek, A., Fuchs, S., Draxler, C., Asu, E.L., Dediu, D., Hiovain, K., et al. (2022). The bouba/kiki effect is robust across cultures and writing systems. Philosophical Transactions of the Royal Society B, 377(1841), p.20200390.

23. Cuskley, C., Simner, J., and Kirby, S. (2017). Phonological and orthographic influences in the bouba-kiki effect. Psychological research, 81(1), pp.119-130.

24. Kawachi, B. (2014). The Sounds of Colors and Tastes: An Experimental Extension of the Bouba Kiki Effect. Central Washington University oral presentation. Available at: https://digitalcommons.cwu.edu/source/2014/cwucenters/1/.

25. Browning, W., & Ryan, C. (2020). Nature Inside: A Biophilic Design Guide. Taylor & Francis, Oxfordshire, UK. doi: 10.4324/9781003033011.

26. Gregory, R.L. (2015). Eye and brain: The psychology of seeing (Vol. 80). Princeton university press.

27. Glikson, A.Y. (2014). Evolution of the atmosphere, fire and the Anthropocene climate event horizon (p. 174). Springer, The Netherlands.

28. Carmody, R.N., and Wrangham, R.W. (2009). The energetic significance of cooking. Journal of human evolution, 57(4), pp.379-391.

29. Shekhar, A., and DiMicco, J.A. (1987). Defense reaction elicited by injection of GABA antagonists and synthesis inhibitors into the posterior hypothalamus in rats. Neuropharmacology, 26(5), pp.407-417.

30. Knox, R. (2010). 'The teen brain: It's just not grown up yet.' National Public Radio. Last accessed at http://www.npr.org/templates/story/story.php.

31. Max Wertheimer (1880-1943), Kurt Koffka (1886-1941), and Wolfgang Köhler (1887-1967)

32. Purves, D., and Lotto, R.B. (2003). Why we see what we do: An empirical theory of vision. Sinauer Associates.

33. Thomson, L.C., and Wright, W.D. (1947). The colour sensitivity of the retina within the central fovea of man. The Journal of physiology, 105(4), p.316.

34. Schiller, P.H., and Tehovnik, E.J. (2001). Look and see: how the brain moves your eyes about. Progress in brain research, 134, pp.127-142.

35. David H. Hubel (1989), Eye, Brain and Vision. New York: Scientific American Library.

36. Marr, D. (1982). Vision: A Computational Investigation into the Human Representation and Processing of Visual Information. San Francisco: W. H. Freeman.

37. Goodale, M.A., Milner, A.D. (1992). Separate visual pathways for perception and action. Trends Neurosci. 15 (1): 20-25. doi:10.1016/0166-2236(92)90344-8. PMID 1374953. S2CID 793980.

38. Park, B.J., Tsunetsugu, Y., Kasetani, T., Hirano, H., Kagawa, T., Sato, M., and Miyazaki, Y. (2007). Physiological effects of shinrin-yoku (taking in the atmosphere of the forest) using salivary cortisol and cerebral activity as indicators. Journal of physiological anthropology, 26(2), pp.123-128.

39. Mandelbrot, B.B. (1982). The fractal geometry of nature (Vol. 1). New York: W.H. Freeman.

40. Turner, M.J. (1998). The origins of fractals. Millennium mathematics project, University of Cambridge. Available at: https://plus.maths.org/issue6/turner1/feat.pdf. Retrieved 15 July 2022.

41. Lovejoy, S., and Mandelbrot, B.B. (1985). Fractal properties of rain, and a fractal model. Tellus A, 37(3), pp.209-232.

42. Barnsley, M.F. (2014). Fractals everywhere. Academic Press.

43. Foster, R.G. (2020). Sleep, circadian rhythms and health. Interface Focus, 10(3), p.20190098.

44. The Endocrine Society 98th annual meeting (2016). Study investigates light, biological clocks, estrogen receptor expression in the breast. Science Daily. Retrieved November 9, 2022 from www.sciencedaily.com/releases/2016/04/160403152327.htm .

45. Berson, D.M. (2003) Strange vision: ganglion cells as circadian photoreceptors. Trends in Neurosciences, 26(6), pp.314-320.

46. Provencio, I., and Foster, R.G. (1995). Circadian rhythms in mice can be regulated by photoreceptors with cone-like characteristics. Brain research, 694(1-2), pp.183-190.

47. Wong, K.Y., Dunn, F.A., Berson, D.M. (2005). Photoreceptor adaptation in intrinsically photosensitive retinal ganglion cells. Neuron, 48(6), pp.1001-1010.

48. Arendt, J., and Broadway, J. (1987). Light and melatonin as zeitgebers in man. Chronobiology international, 4(2), pp.273-282.

49. Smolensky, M.H., Sackett-Lundeen, L.L., and Portaluppi, F. (2015). Nocturnal light pollution and underexposure to daytime sunlight: Complementary mechanisms of circadian disruption and related diseases. Chronobiology international, 32(8), pp.1029-1048.

50. Gomes, C.C., and Preto, S. (2015). Blue light: A blessing or a curse? Procedia Manufacturing, 3, pp.4472-4479.

51. Dr Shelley James (2022) How can space station lighting help us here on earth? | Dr Shelley James | TEDxNorthwich. Available at: https://www.youtube.com/watch?v=YMvIL1p6Z1k(Accessed 10 November, 2022).

52. McAuliffe, S. (2022). The Benefits Of Natural Light In The Workplace. Available at: https://www.cantifix.co.uk/blog/benefits-of-natural-light-in-the-workplace/. (Accessed 10 November, 2022).

53. Zerbini, G., Kantermann, T., and Merrow, M. (2020). Strategies to decrease social jetlag: reducing evening blue light advances sleep and melatonin. European Journal of Neuroscience, 51(12), pp.2355-2366.

54. Ecker, J.L., Dumitrescu, O.N., Wong, K.Y., Alam, N.M., Chen, S.K., LeGates, T., et al. (2010). Melanopsin-expressing retinal ganglion-cell photoreceptors: cellular diversity and role in pattern vision. Neuron. 67 (1), pp. 49-60.

55. Travis, R.C., Balkwill, A., Fensom, G.K., Appleby, P.N., Reeves, G.K., Wang, X.S., et al. (2016). Night shift work and breast cancer incidence: three prospective studies and meta-analysis of published studies. JNCI: Journal of the National Cancer Institute, 108(12), p.djw169.

56. Lévi, F. (2001). Circadian chronotherapy for human cancers. The lancet oncology, 2(5), pp.307-315.

57. Long, J.E., Drayson, M.T., Taylor, A.E., Toellner, K.M., Lord, J.M., and Phillips, A.C. (2016). Morning vaccination enhances antibody response over afternoon vaccination: a cluster-randomised trial. Vaccine, 34(24), pp.2679-2685.

58. Hermida, R.C., et al. (2020). Bedtime hypertension treatment improves cardiovascular risk reduction: the Hygia Chronotherapy Trial European Heart Journal. 41(48) pp. 4565-4576. doi: 10.1093/eurheartj/ehz754.

59. Hermida, R.C., et al. (2018). Asleep blood pressure: significant prognostic marker of vascular risk and therapeutic target for intervention Hygia project. European Heart Journal, 39, pp. 4159-4171. doi:10.1093/eurheartj/ehy475.

60. Kumar, P.V.A., Dakup, P.P., Sarkar, S., Modasia, J.B., Motzner, M.S., and Gaddameedhi, S. (2019). Focus: Clocks and Cycles: It's About Time: Advances in Understanding the Circadian Regulation of DNA Damage and Repair in Carcinogenesis and Cancer Treatment Outcomes. The Yale Journal of Biology and Medicine, 92(2), p.305.

61. Reilly, T., Atkinson, G., Edwards, B., Waterhouse, J., Farrelly, K. and Fairhurst, E. (2007). Diurnal variation in temperature, mental and physical performance, and tasks specifically related to football (soccer). Chronobiology international, 24(3), pp. 507-519.

62. Roenneberg, T. (2012). What is chronotype? Sleep and biological rhythms, 10(2), pp.75-76.

63. Tarlach, G. (2017). Chronotypes: Evolution Explains Night Owls and Early Birds. Available at: https://www.discovermagazine.com/planet-earth/chronotypes-evolution-explains-night-owls-and-early-birds (Accessed: 9 November 2022).

64. Breus, M. (2016). The Power of When: Discover Your Chronotype and Maximise Your Potential. Random House.

65. At What Age Can Babies See Color? (2022) Available at: https://www.nvisioncenters.com/childrens-eye-health/babies-see-color/№:~:text=Babies%20%26%20Color%20Vision,-Babies%20can%20tell&text=Newborns%20can%20see%20contrast%20between,3%20and%204%20months%20old. (Accessed: 10 November, 2022).

66. Benitez-Quiroz, C.F., Srinivasan, R., Martinez, A.M. (2018). Facial color is an efficient mechanism to visually transmit emotion. Proc. Natl. Acad. Sci. USA 115, pp. 3581-3586.

67. Lim, S. (2011). Phototherapy and the benefits of LEDs. Journal of the Society for Information Display, 19(12), pp. 882-887.

68. Bennett, C.P., Hague, A., and Perkins, C. (1991). The use of Baker-Miller pink in police operational and university experimental situations in Britain. International Journal of Biosocial & Medical Research, 13(1), pp. 118-127.

69. Schauss, A. (1979). Tranquilizing Effect of Color Reduces Aggressive Behavior and Potential Violence. Available at: https://isom.ca/wp-content/uploads/2020/01/JOM_1979_08_4_01_Tranquilizing_Effect_of_Color_Reduces_Aggressive-.pdf (Accessed 9 November, 2022).

70. Hambly, Bob (2018). Baker-Miller Pink. Available at: https://www.colourstudies.com/blog/2017/5/3/baker-miller-pink (Accessed 9 November, 2022).

71. Ziegler, M. (2018). Sky Bet Championship: Norwich City paint away dressing room pink to decrease opposition testosterone. Available at: https://www.thetimes.co.uk/article/sky-bet-championship-norwich-city-paint-away-dressing-room-pink-to-decrease-opposition-testosterone-v2fjrb0m6 (Accessed 10 November 2022).

72. Li, W.H., Seo, I., Kim, B., Fassih, A., Southall, M.D., and Parsa, R. (2021). Low level red plus near infrared lights combination induces expressions of collagen and elastin in human skin in vitro. International Journal of Cosmetic Science, 43(3), pp.311-320.

73. Chellappa SL, Ly JQ, Meyer C, et al. (2014). Photic memory for executive brain responses. Proc Natl Acad Sci USA. 111(16), pp. 6087-6091. doi:10.1073/pnas.1320005111

74. Fritsch, C., Stege, H., Saalmann, G., Goerz, G., Ruzicka, T. and Krutmann, J. (1997). Green light is effective and less painful than red light in photodynamic therapy of facial solar keratoses. Photodermatology, Photoimmunology & Photomedicine, 13(5□6), pp.181-185.

75. Martin, L., Porreca, F., Mata, E.I., Salloum, M., Goel, V., Gunnala, P., et al. (2021). Green light exposure improves pain and quality of life in fibromyalgia patients: a preliminary one-way crossover clinical trial. Pain Medicine, 22(1), pp.118-130.

76. Kaiyan Medical. Therapeutic and Aesthetic Uses of Blue & Red Light Therapy Together. Available at: https://www.kaiyanmedical.com/post/therapeutic-and-aesthetic-uses-of-blue-red-light-therapy-together

77. Gomez, F., Gomez, G. (2018). Violet-blue Light and Streptococcus mutans Biofilm-induced Carious Lesions. Dentistry School theses and dissertations, Indiana University-Purdue University Indianapolis.

78. Stern, M., Broja, M., Sansone, R., Gröne, M., Skene, S.S., et al. (2018). Blue light exposure decreases systolic blood pressure, arterial stiffness, and improves endothelial function in humans. European journal of preventive cardiology, 25(17), pp.1875-1883.

79. Clark, L.A. (1978). The Ancient Art of Color Therapy. Connecticut, USA: Devin-Adair Co. 1st Ed 1975.

80. Wills, P. (1993). Colour Therapy. The Use of Colour for Health and Healing. Dorset, U.K.: Element Books.

81. Walker, M. (1991): The Power of Color. New York, USA: Avery Publishing Group.

82. Sims, P. (2022). What is Melanopic Lux? Available at: https://luminusdevices.zendesk.com/hc/en-us/articles/4409858873229-What-is-Melanopic-Lux- (Accessed on 8 November, 2022)

83. Dangol, R. (2011). Colour Rendering Index and colour rendering of LEDs. Master's thesis, Aalto University, Finland.

84. Atchison, D.A., Smith, G., and Smith, G. (2000). Optics of the human eye Vol. 35. Oxford: Butterworth-Heinemann.

85. Charman, W.N. (2008). The eye in focus: accommodation and presbyopia. Clinical and experimental optometry, 91(3), pp. 207-225.

86. De Lepeleire, J., Bouwen, A., De Coninck, L., and Buntinx, F. (2007). Insufficient lighting in nursing homes. Journal of the American Medical Directors Association, 8(5), pp. 314-317.

87. Zanoli, S.M., and Barchiesi, D. (2012). Thermal and lighting control system with energy saving and users comfort features. In 2012 20th Mediterranean Conference on Control & Automation (MED), pp. 1322-1327). Institute of Electrical and Electronic Engineers (IEEE).

88. Gatersleben, B., and Andrews, M. (2013). When walking in nature is not restorative The role of prospect and refuge. Health & place, 20, pp. 91-101.

89. Kitsinelis, S., Arexis-Boisson, L., Zhang, Y., and Zissis, G. (2013). LED flicker: A drawback or an opportunity? Optics and Photonics Journal, 3(1).

90. Wilkins, A., Veitch, J., and Lehman, B. (2010). LED lighting flicker and potential health concerns: IEEE standard PAR1789 update. In 2010 IEEE Energy Conversion Congress and Exposition (pp. 171-178).

91. Wilkins, A.J. (2017). The scientific reason you don't like LED bulbs – and the simple way to fix them. theconversation.com. Retrieved 3 August 2021.

92. Buck, S. (2017). During a 1994 blackout, LA residents called 911 when they saw the Milky Way for the first time. Available at: https://timeline.com/los-angeles-light-pollution-ebd60d5acd43. (Accessed on 8 November 2022).

93. Cooper, K. (2022). LED streetlights are increasing blue-light pollution in Europe. Available at https://physicsworld.com/a/led-streetlights-are-increasing-blue-light-pollution-in-europe/. (Accessed on 9 November 2022)

94. Kellert, S. and Calabrese, E. (2015). The practice of biophilic design. www.biophilic-design.com, p.21.

Section 3: How to design biophilically, with a focus on artificial lighting.

1. Browning, W., & Ryan, C. (2020). Nature Inside: A Biophilic Design Guide. Taylor & Francis, Oxfordshire, UK. doi: 10.4324/9781003033011.

2. Beauchamp, M.S., Lee, K.E., Haxby, J.V., and Martin, A. (2003). fMRI Responses to Video and Point-Light Displays of Moving Humans and Manipulable Objects. Journal of Cognitive Neuroscience, 15(7), pp. 991-1001.

3. Nicol and Humphreys (2002). Adaptive Thermal Comfort and Sustainable Thermal Standards for Buildings. Oxford Centre for Sustainable Development, School of Architecture, Oxford Brookes University, Oxford.

4. Biederman, I., and Vessel, E. (2006). Perceptual pleasure and the brain. American Scientist 94(3), p. 247.

5. Clanton, N. (2014). Opinion: Light pollution... is it important? Lighting Research and Technology, 46(1), p.4.

6. Joye, Y. (2007) Architectural Lessons from Environmental Psychology: The Case of Biophilic Architecture. Review of General Psychology, 11(4), pp.305-328.

7. Vessel, Edward A. (2012). New York University Center for Brain Imaging. Personal communication with the authors. 82

8. Thompson, D'A.W. (1917). On growth and form. First edn. Cambridge University Press.

9. This is labelled as ref [8] in your text, I assume it comes from the browning book

10. Similarly this is labelled as ref [10]

11. Salingaros, N. (2012). Fractal Art and Architecture Reduce Physiological Stress. Journal of Bio-Urbanism, 2, pp.11-28.

12. Dosen, A.S., and Ostwald, M.J. (2013). Prospect and Refuge Theory: Constructing a Critical Definition for Architecture and Design. The International Journal of Design in Society 6(1), pp. 9-24. doi:10.18848/2325-1328/CGP/v06i01/38559.

13. Hildebrand (1991).

14. Grahn, P., and Stigsdotter, U.K. (2010). The relation between perceived sensory dimensions of urban green space and stress restoration. Landscape and Urban Planning, 94(3-4), pp.264-275.

15. Wang and Taylor (2006).

16. Petherick, N. (2000). Environmental Design and Fear: The Prospect-Refuge Model and the University College of the Cariboo Campus. Western Geography, 10/11, pp. 89-112.

17. Ulrich, R.S. (1993). Biophilia, biophobia, and natural landscapes. The biophilia hypothesis, 7, pp.73-137.

18. Kaplan, R., and Kaplan, S. (1989). The Experience of Nature: A Psychological Perspective. New York: Cambridge University Press.

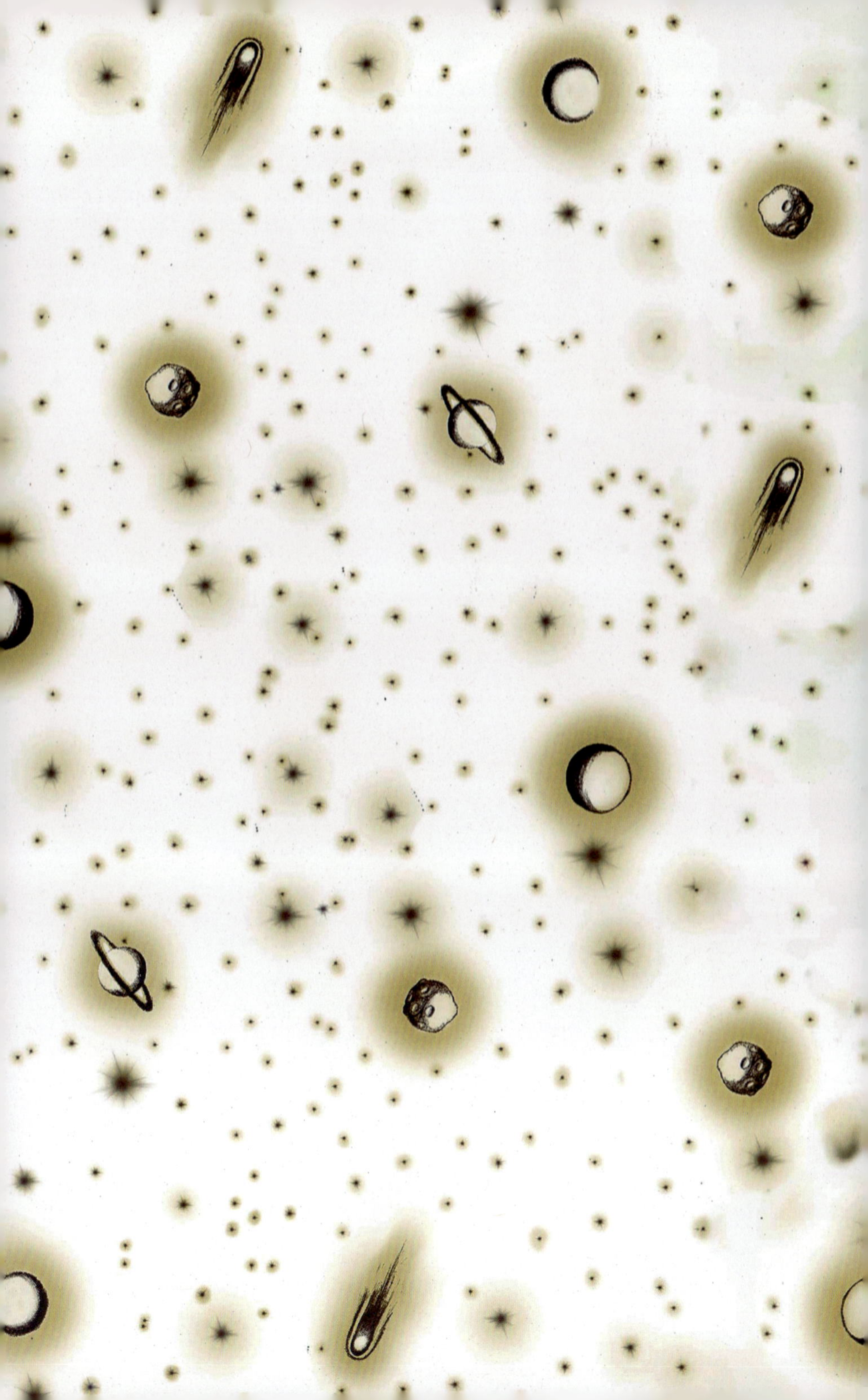

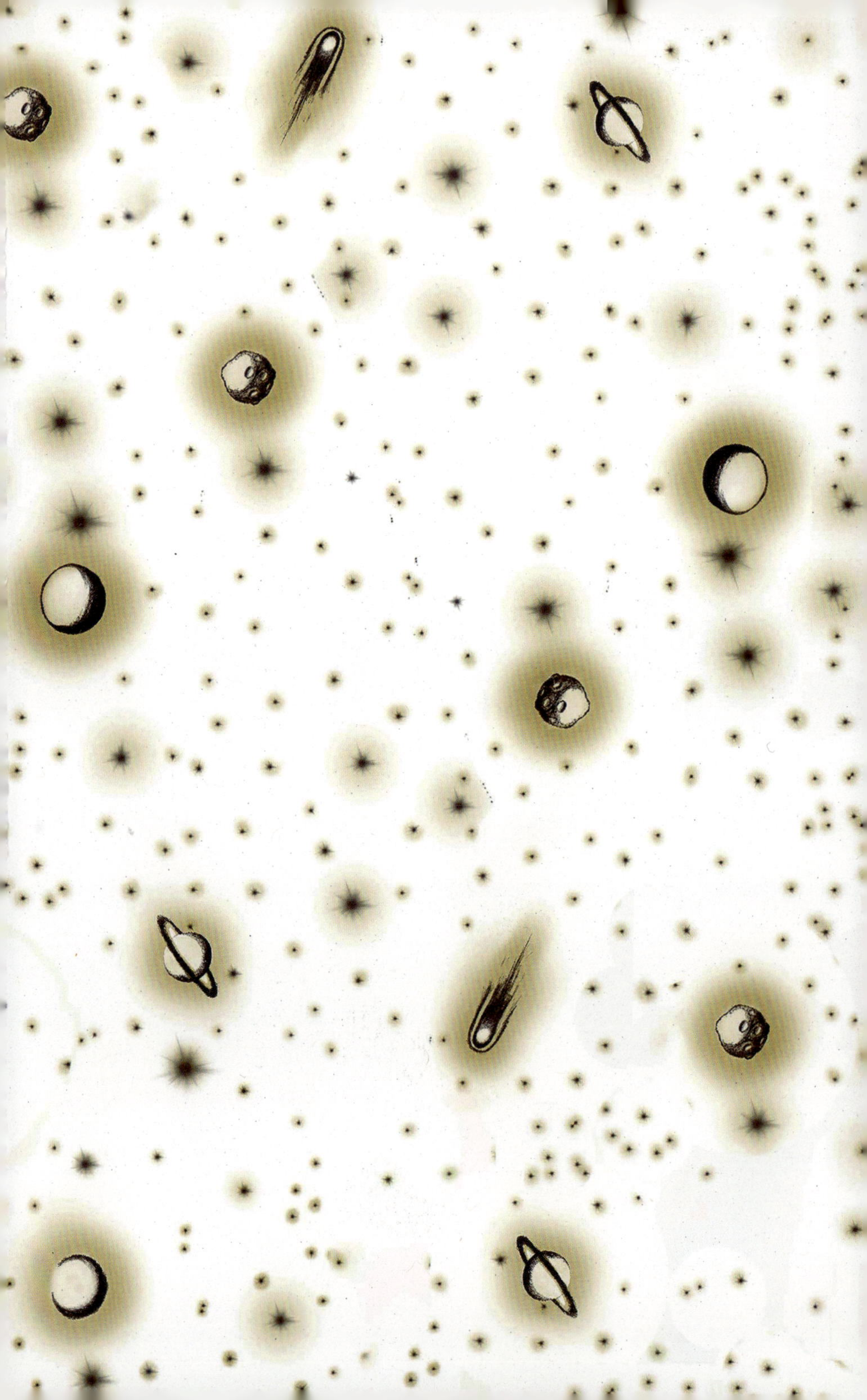